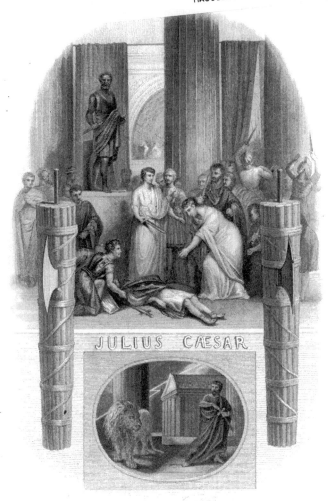

JULIUS CAESAR

ENJOY SHAKESPEARE

Julius Caesar
King Lear
Macbeth
Much Ado About Nothing
Romeo and Juliet
Twelfth Night

Check for coming titles at www.FullMeasurePress.com

ENJOY SHAKESPEARE

Julius Caesar

By

William Shakespeare

A Verse Translation

By

Kent Richmond

 Full Measure Press • Lakewood, California

Published by
Full Measure Press
P.O. Box 6294
Lakewood, Calif. 90714-6294 USA

For ordering information visit www.FullMeasurePress.com

ISBN-13, print ed.   978-0-9836379-0-5
ISBN-10, print ed.   0-9836379-0-3

First Printing

Printed in the United States of America

Contents

Illustrations

Front matter illustration and illustration on page 123 from *Galerie des Personage de Shakspeare* (1844), compiled by Amédée Pichot (1795-1877). Paris: Baudry, Librairie Européenne.

From Clipart.com: page 17, originally from *Cassell's Illustrated Universal History—Rome* (1890); page 30 "Caesar and his Train" by Max Adamo (1857-1901); page 76, detail from the "Assassination of Caesar" (1887) by Georges Rochegrosse (1852-1938); page 95, and page 166.

Page 43, from "Mr. Jamieson as Brutus" by Martin and Johnson (1855) from *The Complete Works of Shakespeare, Vol. II, Tragedies.* (1878). Philadelphia: William T. Amies.

Pages 46 and 121 from *The Tragedy of Julius Caesar* (1872), edited with notes by William J. Rolfe. New York: Harper and Brothers.

Page 69 and 163 from *The Royal Shakespeare* (1894). London, Paris, and Melbourne: Cassell and Company Limited. Page 69, from "Caesar and Calpurnia" by Frank Dicksee (1853-1928), engraved by J. Bauer; page 154 "The Globe Theatre, 1613" by Percival Skelton (1800-1900), engraved by John Godfrey (1817-1889).

Page 99 from *Julius Caesar* (1913). New York: World Book Company. "Mark Antony's Funeral Oration Over the Corpse of Caesar" by Heinrich Spiess (1832-1875).

About this Translation

This translation makes the language of William Shakespeare's *Julius Caesar* more contemporary without modernizing the play in any other way. No lines are omitted or simplified, and no characters or scenes are deleted.

My aim is for readers to experience Shakespeare's plays with the level of challenge and comprehension offered to audiences 400 years ago. Despite the richness of the plays, theatergoers in that era did not need scene summaries to follow the plot, footnotes to interpret vocabulary, or elaborate gestures to help them recognize a joke or guess at a character's intentions or emotional state. After all, Shakespeare's characters tell us what they are thinking. The plays lasted only a couple of hours, which means the actors spoke at a fairly rapid, though comfortable, pace.

To qualify this translation as authentic Shakespeare, I preserve the metrical rhythm of the original as much as possible. When the original employs iambic pentameter, this translation does too. When characters speak in prose, the translation shifts to prose. Rhymes, the occasional alliteration, and metrical irregularities remain. Jokes, inspired or lame, and poetic devices get modern equivalents. Sentence length and syntactic complexity are the same.

To help comprehension, I occasionally add brief pieces of exposition, careful to operate within the metrical constraints imposed by the original. Shakespeare occasionally makes references to Greek mythology, historical figures, and folk legends, many of which are obscure today. So "Pompey's blood" becomes "Pompey's sons," or "Pompey's Porch" becomes "the colonnade/ at Pompey's theatre." This practice eliminates the need for footnotes, which are unavailable to the theatre audience and a distraction to readers. The occasional endnote may add historical information, offer an alternate translation of a disputed passage, or explain a decision to deviate from the original. Readers can ignore endnotes without loss of comprehension.

I suggest reading the translation without referring to the original so that you can imagine the play as theatre in real time with the rhythm and pacing undisturbed. Don't be surprised if the "colors" seem a bit brighter than you remember them. After four centuries, more than a little "linguistic grime" builds up as our language changes. Keep in mind how surprised we are when Renaissance paintings are restored to their original state and those muted, sepia hues turn into celebrations of color. My translation wants you to see the same colors that the groundlings and the royalty saw when they crowded into theatres 400 years ago.

Kent Richmond
Lakewood, California

Notes on the Meter

Shakespeare's plays mix blank verse (unrhymed iambic pentameter), prose, and songs. They also include couplets or other rhyme schemes to close scenes and heighten dramatic exchanges. This translation preserves these forms, assuming Shakespeare had a dramatic justification for these swings between blank verse, prose, and rhyme.

Shakespeare's blank verse can become quite complex and requires decisions as to what constitutes a metrical line. *Julius Caesar*, for example, is full of short lines, long lines (21 hexameters, in fact), shared lines, lines with extra syllables, and other deviations from the expected ten-syllable line. If a line deviates, was Shakespeare sloppy? Is the text corrupt? Has the pronunciation changed? Or was Shakespeare aiming for some dramatic effect?

Shakespeare did not leave us polished editions of his plays. But several hundred years of tinkering by scholars has provided the polishing and copy editing that Shakespeare failed to do. I take advantage of that scholarship and assume that any remaining anomalies are part of Shakespeare's design and must be respected. If the deviant meter is due to pronunciation change, then I find a metrical equivalent in contemporary English. If not, then the translation deviates in the same way as the original. Of course no translation can perfectly capture both the sense and sound of poetry. When conflicts arise, I favor sense over strict adherence to the rhythm. Yet I do not allow a line to have a rhythm not found in Shakespeare's verse at the time he wrote the play.

For more information on Shakespeare's blank verse, see my article " How Iambic Pentameter Works" accompanying my translations of *Twelfth Night* and *Macbeth*.

About the Play

*J*ulius Caesar, the first of Shakespeare's great tragedies, was most likely one of the first productions staged at the Globe Theatre after it opened in 1599. This theatre, with a large area around the stage for patrons to stand and watch, would have been a perfect venue for the raucous crowd scenes and rousing speeches that are the highlight of the play. Imagine Mark Antony with his "Friends, Romans, countrymen, lend me your ears" inviting an audience of several thousand to be part of the spectacle (see Appendix 2 for more on the Globe).

The historical events in *Julius Caesar* took place 1600 years before Shakespeare's birth, yet the story was by no means obscure. Roman history was an important school subject, and Shakespeare was tackling the most famous event in pre-Christian Europe—the brutal, controversial assassination of Caesar by a cabal of Roman senators led by Marcus Brutus. Based primarily on information gleaned from Thomas North's translation of *Plutarch's Lives* (1579), Shakespeare's dramatic rendering has kept the controversy surrounding Caesar's death alive for at least another 400 years. Today the play is standard reading in countless schools, where students take sides in mock debates. Was Brutus a hero motivated by love of freedom and democracy who rid Rome of an arrogant tyrant? Or was he a misguided, ungrateful blunderer who pointlessly killed a brilliant military commander, reformer, and author, a man who brought order and power to Rome and invented the calendar we use today?

To better appreciate the play's complexities, the modern reader may benefit from a review of events preceding the play's action. Shakespeare—so adept at combining events and compressing time—makes it seem as if the story happened over a long holiday weekend. The actual events spread over about six years, from 48 BC to 42 BC, a period marked by revolutionary change in the way Rome was governed.

For several centuries, Rome had operated as a republic with a system of checks and balances that limited an individual politician's power. Both aristocrats (patricians) and commoners (plebeians) had representation and institutions to protect their interests. No one could be crowned king, and legislative, judicial, and administrative control was spread among a complex array of institutions including the Senate and various councils. Politicians held a variety of positions such as consuls, magistrates, patrician senators, and tribunes of the plebeians. To reduce the threat of military takeover, generals were not allowed near the vicinity of Rome without first disbanding their armies north of the Rubicon river in eastern Italy. Crossing the Rubicon with an army was punished by death.

In 133 BC, plagued by nepotism, corruption, and poverty, the Roman republic became unstable. One source of conflict, relevant to Shakespeare's play, was increased rivalry between patricians and plebeians. Ambitious politicians could gain support by making promises to plebeians, a situation that limited the power of Senate patricians while making plebeians more and more dependent on Rome. In the play, we see or hear of characters seeking popular support by promising to spread largesse, most memorably when Mark Antony reads Caesar's will. We also learn that Marcus Brutus and other aristocratic senators fear and resent losing power to these politicians. Brutus believes himself to be a descendent of Lucius Junius Brutus, who according to legend, drove Tarquinius Superbus, the last of the ancient kings, out of Rome in the sixth century BC. He is proud of that heritage and wants Rome to remain a republic run by a noble elite, not a popular king.

The play opens with two tribunes scolding tradesmen for being too fickle in their loyalties. These shifting loyalties grew out of an event that happened in 59 BC. Three powerful rivals—Julius Caesar, Marcus Crassus, and Pompeius Magnus (Pompey the Great)—formed an unofficial alliance, or triumvirate, to share power. The triumvirate temporarily brought stability to Rome while reducing the power of the aristocratic and conservative Senate. During the next decade, Caesar set out to conquer western Europe, invading Britain twice and cementing Roman control of Gaul (now western Europe). Caesar's success and the death of Crassus in the Parthian wars in 53 BC doomed the triumvirate. Pompey worked to undermine and limit Caesar's power, so in 49 BC Caesar defied Roman law and crossed the Rubicon with his army and marched toward Rome. Pompey abandoned Rome, and in 48 BC lost a battle to Caesar's forces in central Greece. Pompey fled to Egypt where he was killed. Now with unrivalled power, Caesar began reforming Roman institutions and was given the title "dictator in perpetuity." Afraid that the popular Caesar would further erode their power, a group of senators led by Marcus Brutus murdered Caesar. Two years later, Brutus was defeated in battle by Mark Antony and Octavius Caesar, who would later become Augustus Caesar.

Shakespeare's condensed version of this history picks up the action right before the murder on March 15, 44 BC. All but three short scenes focus on the thoughts, intimate moments, and public actions of three central characters—Marcus Brutus, a highly respected and serious magistrate and senator; Cassius, an impulsive, hot-blooded senator who convinces Brutus to lead the conspiracy; and Mark Antony, a fun-loving and gifted opportunist who remains loyal to Caesar. A fourth major character—Caesar himself—surprisingly has only a supporting role in the play. He appears just four times and rarely in a flattering light. We see him hampered by deafness and fainting spells, rattled by superstitions, fooled by flattery, and harried by Calpurnia, his understandably fearful wife. The sarcastic Casca recounts for Brutus and Cassius a public speech that we do not hear and makes Caesar seem shameless, clownish, and feeble. Is Shakespeare building sympathy for the conspirators? In the *Divine Comedy*, the Italian poet Dante confined Brutus and Cassius to the very center of hell. Is Shakespeare offering a rebuttal, a piece of pro-Brutus propaganda?

As the play proceeds, Shakespeare forces us to alter our initial assessments of these four characters. Brutus, described even by his enemy Mark Antony, as the "noblest Roman of them all" seems a thoughtful, idealistic man, tender toward his wife and servants, eloquent in his self-analysis, loyal to and admired by friends. He is motivated by an honest desire to reestablish a republican Rome and preempt abuses by a too powerful Caesar. Yet the failure of his enterprise seems inevitable. At Caesar's funeral, "Caesar's angel," as Mark Antony mockingly calls Brutus, delivers an explanation (in prose, not verse) for his actions that sounds convincing enough but is too spare and unemotional to convince the crowd for long. Philosophically a stoic, Brutus is proud of how much grief and responsibility he can endure, but he keeps his thoughts and burdens to himself, isolating himself from intimates, most tellingly from Portia, his perceptive wife. His mulishness and self-reliance lead him to dismiss sound advice.

Cassius, second only to Brutus in the number of lines he speaks, differs sharply in motive and character from his more honorable friend. Caesar, showing his political astuteness, senses this difference and tells Mark Antony that Cassius has a "lean and hungry look. He thinks too much. Such men are dangerous." In seeking justification for the coup, Cassius' arguments are emotional, personal, and weird. Caesar is not a strong swimmer, he says, and Caesar once whined for water when he had a fever. In this way, Cassius sows discontent and resentment without actually addressing Caesar's skills as a leader. Sensing Brutus is not convinced, Cassius shows his deceitful side by sending him fake letters suggesting there is widespread popular support for Brutus to lead a coup. And during the closing battle, we see Brutus' stiff-upper-lip stoicism at work while the emotionally volatile and panicky Cassius, despite being the better military strategist, crumples under the pressure. Though the sins of Cassius are many, he still can surprise us with how right he can be. He warns Brutus about letting Mark Antony speak at Caesar's funeral and tells Brutus in Act Five to have his troops hold the high ground and let the battle come to him. Ignoring Cassius' advice costs Brutus dearly.

Mark Antony is assigned the two most famous speeches in the play, his "dogs of war" speech and his crowd-stirring eulogy for Caesar. Athletic and charismatic, the life of every party, he uses his talents to spark an immediate rebellion against Brutus. He then forms a new triumvirate with Octavius and Lepidus to rule Rome and march against Brutus and Cassius. As impressive as he is in displaying Caesar as a victim of vicious betrayal at the funeral, we soon witness a darker side. We already know that he is prone to misjudgment when he tells Caesar not to fear Cassius. He then moves too far in the opposite direction by executing and banishing men not involved in the assassination. He even dupes the weakest member of the triumvirate, Lepidus, into taking the heat for deciding who to punish. Antony wants to rule Rome, yet Shakespeare's audience in 1599 knew that the taciturn Octavius, the sole heir to Caesar's name and wealth, will prove more adept at seizing power and a decade later defeat Antony in battle. Shakespeare dramatizes the events leading to Antony's demise in the play's sequel, *Antony and Cleopatra.*

Shakespeare makes sure we are not comfortable with our first impressions of Brutus, Cassius, and Antony. Is this also the case with Caesar? In the first half of the play, Shakespeare lets characters denigrate Caesar without rebuttal, yet beginning with Mark Antony's eulogy at his funeral, we sense Caesar had leadership qualities that the coup's leaders lack and a sway over others that does not end with his murder. His stature becomes increasingly apparent as Brutus and Cassius ready for a showdown with the forces out to avenge Caesar's death. Their famous quarrel in Act Four reveals that corruption fostered by Cassius is weakening their cause but also that Brutus is too high-minded to make the political accommodations necessary for success. Caesar in his prime clearly handled power better. Brutus believes his actions are motivated by his deep love for Rome's republic, but these noble thoughts and aims are belied by the unpopularity of his cause within and outside Rome. He is dogged not only by Caesar's former followers but by Caesar's ghost as well. Brutus and Cassius are battling armies led by Octavius and Antony, yet their closing lines call out to Caesar, whose greatness they must acknowledge.

Shakespeare wrote *Julius Caesar* knowing that Queen Elizabeth was aging and most likely near the end of her long reign. Since she had named no successor, there were concerns that England would descend into chaos as the scramble to crown a new monarch began. Shakespeare had cut his teeth as a dramatist on a series of plays about the Wars of the Roses (1455-1485) when England was torn by dynastic wars and had seven different kings. Later plays suggest that civil war is the unfavorable and inevitable outcome of regicide (*Macbeth*) or irresponsible abnegation *(King Lear)*. In this light, it seems that Shakespeare's sympathies would lean away from Brutus and toward supporting a powerful central monarch such as Julius Caesar. Yet readers and theatergoers often identify strongly with Brutus, and productions have been known to stack the deck by removing lines that make Brutus look unfavorable. The 1937 Mercury Theatre production under the direction of Orson Welles demonized Caesar by imagining him as a Mussolini-like fascist trading Nazi salutes with his followers. Certainly *Julius Caesar* must owe part of its lasting popularity to its ambiguity and Shakespeare's amazing ability to play with our sympathies without tipping his hand.

Characters in the Play

JULIUS CAESAR
CALPURNIA, his wife

Marcus **BRUTUS**, praetor (magistrate) of Rome *,honor*
PORTIA, his wife
LUCIUS, his personal servant

Caius **CASSIUS**, co-conspirator with Brutus *, jealous, overly confident*
PINDARUS, a servant to Cassius

Other Patricians Conspiring against Caesar
CASCA
TREBONIUS
Caius **LIGARIUS**
DECIUS Brutus
METELLUS Cimber
CINNA

Triumvirate Ruling Rome After Act 3
MARK ANTONY, friend of Caesar
OCTAVIUS Caesar, great-nephew of Caesar
Aemilius **LEPIDUS**

Other Senators
CICERO
PUBLIUS
POPILIUS Lena

Tribunes of the Plebeians
FLAVIUS
MARULLUS

Officers Serving under Brutus and Cassius
LUCILIUS
TITINIUS
MESSALA

15

young **CATO**
STRATO
LABEO
FLAVIUS

Soldiers Serving under Brutus and Cassius
VARRO
CLITUS
CLAUDIUS
DARDANIUS
VOLUMNIUS

a **CARPENTER**
a **COBBLER**
ARTEMIDORUS, a teacher of rhetoric
SOOTHSAYER, a fortune-teller
CAESAR'S GHOST
POET, also named Cinna
another **POET**, in the camp near Sardis

Other **SENATORS, PLEBEIANS, SOLDIERS, SERVANTS,** and **MESSENGERS**

SCENE

Rome
Sardis (now part of Turkey)
The Plains of Philippi (in Macedonia)

Julius Caesar

Act One

Act One

[Enter FLAVIUS, MARULLUS, and a throng of PLE-
BEIANS (including a CARPENTER and a COBBLER),
meeting on a street]

FLAVIUS (a tribune of the plebeians)
Go home, you idle creatures, get on home!
Is this a holiday? What? Don't you know
That tradesmen aren't allowed to walk around
On working days without the tools and clothes
Of their profession? Speak, what is your trade?   5

CARPENTER
Why, sir, a carpenter.

MARULLUS (a tribune of the plebeians)
Where is your leather apron? And your ruler?
Why do you have your best apparel on?
You, sir, what is your trade?

COBBLER
Truly, sir, compared with these fine workmen, I merely   10
cobble at my trade.

MARULLUS
But at what trade? Just give me a straight answer.

COBBLER
A trade, sir, that I hope I can practice with good conscience,
for indeed, sir, I mend bad soles.

19

MARULLUS
What trade, you knave? You no-good knave, what trade?   15

COBBLER
Please, I beg you, don't be sore, but if you're sore, sir, I can
fix you.

MARULLUS
What do you mean by that, you nasty fellow? Fix me?

COBBLER
Fix your shoes, sir.

FLAVIUS
So you're a cobbler, are you?   20

COBBLER
Truly, sir, I make my living punching holes in leather. I
never meddle in another tradesman's affairs, nor those of
women, except with my punch. I truly am, sir, a surgeon to
old pieces of hide. When they are in great danger, I make
them feel like new. The finest men that have ever trod upon   25
the skin of a cow have slipped into my handiwork.

FLAVIUS
But why are you not in your shop today?
Why do you lead these people through the streets?

COBBLER
I'm hoping, sir, to wear out their shoes to get myself more
work. Actually, sir, we've declared a holiday to see Caesar's   30
victory parade and rejoice in his triumph.

MARULLUS
But why rejoice? What conquest could you mean?
What tribute-paying hostages chained to
His chariot wheels has he brought back to Rome?
You blocks, you stones—worse than oblivious!   35
O such hard hearts. Don't you cruel men of Rome
Remember Pompey?[1] Think how many times

You've climbed high up the walls and battlements,
To towers and windows, even chimney tops,
Your infants in your arms, and there you've sat   40
The whole day long in patient expectation
To see great Pompey drive the streets of Rome.
And when you saw his chariot appear,
Did you not shout in unison so loud
That underneath her banks the Tiber trembled,   45
Reverberating when she heard your sounds
Ring out across her sloping shores?
And now you dress up in your best attire?
And now arrange to have a holiday?
And now you toss some flowers in the path   50
Of one who triumphed over Pompey's sons?
Be gone!
Run to your houses, fall upon your knees,
And pray the gods delay whatever plague
Will no doubt punish this ingratitude.   55

FLAVIUS
Go, go, good countrymen. For this offense,
Assemble all the poor men of your rank,
Lead them to Tiber's banks, and let your tears
Flow down it's channel, till the lowest stream
Can rise to kiss the highest shores of all.   60

[Exit PLEBEIANS]

Note how the lowest specimen is touched.
They vanish from us tongue-tied in their guilt.
You take that route down towards the Capitol.
I'll go this way. Strip all the statues clean
Of any decorations that you find.   65

MARULLUS
Is that allowed?
They're for the festival—the Lupercalia.[2]

FLAVIUS
That's no concern. Make sure no statue's hung

With Caesar's plunder. I will roam about
And get the common people off the streets.   70
You do that too, wherever they have massed.
These growing feathers plucked from Caesar's wings
Will keep him at an ordinary height,
Within the sight of men, so we won't live
In servile fear that he'll swoop down on us.   75

[Exit]

Scene Two. Rome. A Public Place

[Trumpets sound. Enter in a procession JULIUS CAE-
SAR, MARK ANTONY (dressed for the race) CALPUR-
NIA, PORTIA, DECIUS Brutus, CICERO, BRUTUS,
CASSIUS, CASCA, a SOOTHSAYER, and a large crowd
of SENATORS, and PLEBEIANS]

JULIUS CAESAR
Calpurnia,—

CASCA (a patrician)
          Silence! Caesar speaks.

[Trumpets cease]

JULIUS CAESAR
                              Calpurnia—

CALPURNIA (Caesar's wife)
Here, my lord.

JULIUS CAESAR
Go stand and block Antonius' path
When he is in the race.—Antonius.

MARK ANTONY (a friend of Caesar)
Caesar, my lord?   5

JULIUS CAESAR
Don't go so fast, Antonius, that you
Forget to touch Calpurnia. Wise men say,
Touching the barren in this holy race
Shakes off the curse of childlessness.

MARK ANTONY
I'll do it.
When Caesar says "Do this," it will be done.   10

JULIUS CAESAR
Proceed. Observe all rites. Leave nothing out.

[Trumpet sounds]

SOOTHSAYER (a fortune-teller)
Caesar!

JULIUS CAESAR
Ha! Who said that?

CASCA
All noise must cease. Be silent once again!

[Trumpet ceases]

JULIUS CAESAR
Who is it in the crowd who's calling me?   15
I hear a voice, shriller than all the music,
Crying out "Caesar!" Speak. Caesar will listen.

SOOTHSAYER
Beware the ides of March.

JULIUS CAESAR
Which man said that?

BRUTUS (praetor of Rome)
A soothsayer says beware the ides of March.

JULIUS CAESAR
Bring him before me. Let me see his face.   20

CASSIUS (a patrician)
You, come out from the crowd. Look up at Caesar.

JULIUS CAESAR
What was it you just said? Speak once again.

SOOTHSAYER
Beware the ides of March.

JULIUS CAESAR
He is a dreamer. Let's ignore him. Go.

[Trumpets sound]
[Exit all except BRUTUS and CASSIUS]

CASSIUS
You wish to see what happens in the race?   25

BRUTUS
Not I.

CASSIUS
Please come and watch.

BRUTUS
I'm not the sporting type. I lack the dose
Of playfulness that Antony must have.
Don't let me, Cassius, hinder your desires.   30
I'll leave now.

CASSIUS
Brutus, I've noticed something recently.
I don't see in your eyes the gentleness
Or show of love that I'm accustomed to.
Your hands are placing reins too harsh and cold   35
Over a loving friend.

BRUTUS
                    Now, Cassius,
Don't be deceived. If my regard for you
Is veiled, it's that I want my troubles kept
Entirely to myself. For I am vexed
These days with feelings quite ambivalent,   40
With thoughts not easily shared with someone else,
Which leave a stain perhaps on my behavior.
My good friends, thus—and, Cassius, you rank first
Among their number—have no cause to fret
And should assume no more from my neglect   45
Than that poor Brutus, warring with himself,
Forgets to show his love to other men.

CASSIUS
Then, Brutus, I was wrong about your feelings,
And due to this have buried in my breast
Important thoughts and serious contemplation.   50
Tell me, good Brutus, can you see your face?

BRUTUS
No, Cassius, for the eye can't see itself
Unless reflected by some other thing.

CASSIUS
That's true,
And it is very much lamented, Brutus,   55
That you have no such mirrors by which to send
Your hidden excellence back toward your eye
So you can see how you appear. I hear
When many of the highest ranked in Rome
(Except "immortal" Caesar) speak of Brutus   60
And groan beneath the yoke we now must wear,
They wish that noble Brutus had their eyes.

BRUTUS
What dangers would you lead me into, Cassius,
That would require that I find in myself
These things that are not in me?   65

CASSIUS
Good Brutus, be prepared for what you'll hear.
And since you know that you can see yourself
The best through your reflection, I, your mirror,
Wish to reveal, without exaggeration,
A part of you which you do not yet know.   70
And do not be suspicious, noble Brutus.
Were I your common clown, or one who's known
To spread his friendship thin by pledging it
To every glad-hander, or if you think
That I will flatter men, and hug them hard   75
And later slander them, or if you think
I'll throw a banquet so the masses know
That I'm their friend, then deem me dangerous.

[Trumpets sound. Shouting is heard]

BRUTUS
What's all this shouting? I'm afraid the people
Are making Caesar king.

CASSIUS
                    Well, if you fear it,   80
Then I must think it's something you don't want.

BRUTUS
I do not, Cassius, though I love him well.
But tell me why you're keeping me so long?
What is it that you wish for me to know?
If any of this talk concerns the public,   85
Show one eye honor and the other death
And I will look on both impartially.
I trust the gods will see to my success
As I love honor more than I fear death.

CASSIUS
I know that this ideal is there inside you   90
As fully as I know your outward features.
Well, honor is the subject of my story.
I cannot tell what you and other men

Think of this life, but if it is up to me,
I'd just as soon not live than live to stand 95
In awe of anyone no better than myself.
I was born free like Caesar; so were you.
We've eaten what he eats, and we can both
Endure the winter's cold as well as he.
One time when on a raw and gusty day 100
The troubled Tiber raged against her shores,
Caesar said, "Right now, Cassius, do you dare
Leap in with me, into this angry flood,
And swim there to that cove?" On hearing this,
Though fully dressed, I plunged right in and called 105
For him to follow, which indeed he did.
The torrent roared, and then we beat it back
With vigorous muscles, thrusting it aside
And parting it, our hearts in competition.
But then before we reached the calmer cove, 110
Caesar cried, "Help me, Cassius, or I'll sink!"
Then like Aeneas, Rome's great forefather,[3]
Whose shoulder saved Anchises from the flames
Of Troy, I took the tired Caesar from
The Tiber's waves. And now I see this man's 115
Become a god, while Cassius has become
A wretched creature bending at the waist
Whenever Caesar throws a glance his way.
He had a fever when he was in Spain;
And when he had a fit, I could observe 120
How hard he shook. It's true! This god was shaking.
His lips, like cowards, fled from their own colors,
And those same eyes whose glance has awed the world
Had lost their luster. I could hear him groan.
Yes, and that tongue of his, which held the Romans 125
Spellbound, whose speeches filled their books,
"Oh, please," it cried, "Give me a drink, Titinius,"
Like some sick girl.—By god, I am amazed
A man of such a feeble constitution
Could grab the lead in this majestic field 130
And cross the line alone.

[Shouting. Trumpets sound]

BRUTUS
                    Is that more cheering?
I have no doubt that this applause must be
For some new honors being heaped on Caesar.

CASSIUS
Why, man, he straddles our thin stretch of world
Like some Colossus, and we puny men   135
Walk under his huge legs and scratch about
To dig ourselves an undistinguished grave.
A man at times is master of his fate.[4]
The fault, dear Brutus, is not in the stars,
But in ourselves—that's why we're underlings.   140
"Brutus" and "Caesar"—what is it that's in "Caesar"?
Why should that name be spoken more than yours?
Write them together, yours is as fine a name;
Say them, it flows as easily from the mouth;
Weigh them, it's just as heavy; cast a spell,   145
"Brutus" will raise a spirit as fast as "Caesar."
Now, in the name of every single god,
Upon what food has Caesar fed that's made
Him grow so huge? This Age we're in's been shamed!
Rome, you have lost your lines of noble blood!   150
And name a time, at least since the great flood,
That's ever been renowned for just one man.
And when, till now, could those who talked of Rome
Claim her wide walks had space for just one man?
Can this be Rome, with all its room to roam,   155
When in it there is but a single man?
O, you and I have heard our fathers say
There was another Brutus long ago[5]
Who would have let the devil govern Rome
Before he'd let a king.   160

BRUTUS
I see no reason to mistrust your friendship.
And where you're pushing me, that I can guess.
The thoughts I've had on this and on these times,
I'll cover in the future. For the moment,
I wish that you—and as a friend I'm begging—   165

Would urge me on no further. What you've said,
I will consider. What you have to say,
I'll calmly listen to and find a time
For both a hearing on these weighty things
And my response. Till then, friend, chew on this: 170
Brutus would rather be some villager
Than list himself among the sons of Rome
And bear the hard conditions that these times
Will likely load on us.

CASSIUS
I'm glad that my weak words   175
Strike even this much spark of fire from Brutus.

BRUTUS
The games are done, and Caesar is returning.

CASSIUS
As they pass by, grab Casca by the sleeve,
He will, sarcastically, I'm sure, tell you
What things of note have taken place today.   180

[Re-enter JULIUS CAESAR and his entourage]

BRUTUS
I'll do so.—But look at this, Cassius.
A mark of anger glows on Caesar's brow,
And all the rest look like they got a scolding.
Calpurnia's cheeks are pale, and Cicero[6]
Glares with a ferret's pointed, fiery eyes   185
The way he does inside the Capitol
When in debate with rival senators.

CASSIUS
Casca will tell us what the trouble is.

JULIUS CAESAR
Antonio.

MARK ANTONY
Caesar?   190

JULIUS CAESAR
Let me have men around me that are fat,
Men with combed hair and such who sleep at night.
Cassius there has a lean and hungry look.
He thinks too much. Such men are dangerous.

MARK ANTONY
Fear him not, Caesar. He's not dangerous.   195
He is a sympathetic, noble Roman.

JULIUS CAESAR
He could be fatter! But I fear him not.
If Caesar's name were given to such fear,
There's no man I'd be sooner to avoid
Than scrawny Cassius there. He reads a lot,   200
He is a great observer, and he sees
Right through men's motives. He does not love plays,
As you do, Antony, cares not for music
And seldom smiles, or smiles in such a way
As if to mock himself and scorn his spirit   205
For being moved to smile at anything.
Men with such hearts can never be at ease
Once they behold one greater than themselves,
And, therefore, they are very dangerous.

I am more apt to state what should be feared   210
Than what I fear, for I am always Caesar.
Come to my right side, for this ear is deaf,
And tell me truly what you think of him.

[Exit CAESAR and his entourage. CASCA stays]

CASCA
You tugged me by my robe. Do you wish to speak with
me?   215

BRUTUS
Yes, Casca. Tell us what occurred today
That's making Caesar look so grim?

CASCA
Why, you were with him, weren't you?

BRUTUS
If so, I would not ask you what occurred.

CASCA
Why, a crown was offered to him, and when offered it, he 220
pushed it away with the back of his hand, like this, and
then the people started cheering.

BRUTUS
What was the second noise for?

CASCA
Why, for that too.

CASSIUS
They cheered him three times. What was the last for?   225

CASCA
Why, for that too.

BRUTUS
Was the crown offered three times?

CASCA
Indeed it was, and he pushed it away three times, each time
gentler than the other, and with each push, the common
folk around me cheered.   230

CASSIUS
Who offered him the crown?

CASCA
Why, Antony.

BRUTUS
Tell us how this was handled, noble Casca.

CASCA
Hang me if I can tell you how it was handled. It was complete nonsense. I ignored it. I saw Mark Antony offer him a   235
crown—not a crown, really. Smaller—one of those coronets.
And as I told you, he pushed it away, though for all I could
tell, he'd have been happy to take it. Then he offered it to
him again. Then he pushed it away again. But to me he
seemed very averse to taking his fingers off of it. And then 240
he offered it a third time. He pushed it away a third time,
and each time he refused it, the rabble cheered and clapped
their calloused hands, and threw their sweaty caps in the
air, and uttered such a great amount of stinking breath
because Caesar refused the crown that Caesar almost suf-   245
focated, for he fainted and fell over when it hit him. And
as for me, I dared not laugh for fear of opening my lips and
breathing the bad air.

CASSIUS
Hold on a minute. You saw Caesar faint?

CASCA
He fell down in the market place and foamed at the mouth   250
and was speechless.

BRUTUS
It's possible. We know he's prone to seizures.

CASSIUS
Not Caesar. You and I and honest Casca—
We are the ones who now may suffer seizure.

CASCA
I don't know what you mean by that, but I am sure that   255
Caesar fell. If the rabble did not clap when he pleased them
or hiss when he displeased them, as they're used to doing
for players in the theatre, then I am not an honest man.

BRUTUS
When he recovered, what did he say then?

CASCA
Indeed, before he fell down, when he realized that the com-   260
mon herd was glad he refused the crown, he popped open
his robe and offered them his throat to cut. If I were a man
of just any occupation and hadn't taken him at his word, I'd
have wanted myself in hell with all the other rogues. And
so he fell. When he came to, he said if he had done or said   265
anything improper, he hoped their worships would realize
it was his illness. Three or four wenches where I stood cried,
"Alas, a good soul!" and forgave him with all their hearts.
But they can't be taken seriously. If Caesar had used his
sword on their mothers, they would have done no less.   270

BRUTUS
And looking so upset, he then came back?

CASCA
Yes.

CASSIUS
Did Cicero say anything?

CASCA
Yes, in Greek.

CASSIUS
For what purpose?   275

CASCA
Well, if I pretended to know that, I could never look you in
the face again. But those that understood him smiled at one
another and shook their heads. I wish I could offer more,
but it was Greek to me. I have other news too. Marullus
and Flavius, for pulling scarves off Caesar's statues, have 280
been removed. Farewell. There was even more nonsense,
if I could remember it.

CASSIUS
Will you dine with me tonight, Casca?

CASCA
No, I have other plans.

CASSIUS
Will you lunch with me tomorrow?   285

CASCA
Yes, if I am alive, and your mind doesn't change, and your
meal's worth eating.

CASSIUS
Good. I will expect you.

CASCA
Do that. Farewell to you both.

[Exit CASCA]

BRUTUS
What a gruff fellow he has grown to be!   290
He had a lively spirit back in school.

CASSIUS
As he still has today when taking on
All kinds of bold or noble enterprises
Though it's well hid behind this sluggish manner.
This coarseness spices up his intellect,   295
Which makes men able to digest his words
And keep their appetites.

BRUTUS
Indeed it does. At this time, I must leave you.
Tomorrow, if you wish to speak with me,
I'll meet you at your house, or if you want,   300
We'll meet at mine, and I will wait for you.

CASSIUS
That's fine. Till then, think of this world we're in.

[Exit Brutus]

Well, Brutus, you are noble, yet I see
Your honorable metal can be wrenched
From what it tends to be. It's fitting then   305
That noble minds stay with those most alike,
For who's so strong he cannot be seduced?
Caesar puts up with me, but he loves Brutus.
If I were Brutus now and he were Cassius,
He would not sway me.[7] I will toss tonight,   310
In different styles of writing, through his windows
As if they came from several citizens,
Letters, all speaking of the great opinion
That Rome has of his name, and indirectly
Caesar's ambition will be hinted at.   315
And after when he thinks his throne's secure,
We'll shake him up, or worse days we'll endure.

[Exit]

Scene Three. Rome. A Street

[Thunder and lightning. Enter, from opposite sides, CAS-
        CA, with his sword drawn, and CICERO]

CICERO (a senator)
Good evening, Casca. Did you take Caesar home?
Why are you out of breath and staring so?

CASCA
Aren't you upset when powers holding sway
Are shaking and unsteady? O Cicero,
I have seen tempests, when the scolding winds   5
Tear knotted oaks apart, and I have seen
The ocean, swelling with ambition, rage
And foam and rise up to the threatening clouds.
But never till tonight, never till now,
Have I gone through a tempest that dropped fire.   10
There's either civil strife up in the heavens,
Or angered by a too defiant world,
The gods now send destruction down on us.

CICERO
Is that the most bewildering thing you saw?

CASCA
A common slave—you'd know him well by sight—   15
Held up his left hand, which caught fire and burned
As bright as twenty torches, yet his hand
Oblivious to the fire remained unscorched.
And then—I've kept my sword drawn ever since—
Right by the Capitol I saw a lion   20
That glared at me and yet went grumbling by
Without attacking me. And huddled in
A heap, I saw a hundred ashen women,
Transformed by fear, who swore to me they saw
Men, all on fire, walk up and down the streets.   25
And yesterday I saw a night owl perch
Itself at noontime in the marketplace,
Hooting and shrieking. When these omens meet
Together all at once, men cannot say
"There has to be some natural cause for this."   30
For I believe these things are ~~ominous,~~ Portentous
A warning to the region where they point.

CICERO
Indeed, the times in which we live are strange.
But men interpret things in their own way,
Removed completely from the thing itself.   35
Is Caesar at the Capitol tomorrow?

CASCA
He is, for he has told Antonio
To send you word that he'll be there tomorrow.

CICERO
Good night then, Casca. This disturbing sky
Is not for walking under.

CASCA
                    Farewell, Cicero.   40

                    [Exit CICERO]
                    [Enter CASSIUS]

CASSIUS
Who's there?

CASCA
          A Roman.

CASSIUS
                    Casca, that's your voice.

CASCA
You have a good ear. Cassius, what a night!

CASSIUS
A pleasing one for honorable men.

CASCA
Who knew the skies could be so menacing?

CASSIUS
Those who have seen an earth this full of faults.   45
And as for me, I've walked around the streets,
In full exposure to this perilous night,
My cloak unfastened, Casca—as you see—
To bare my bosom to the thunderbolts.
And when the jagged streaks of lightning seemed   50

To split the breast of heaven, I placed myself
Directly where the flash of it was aimed.

CASCA
Why would you test the heavens in this way?
It is the role of men to fear and tremble,
When heaven's mightiest gods through signs like these   55
Send ominous messengers to cause dismay.

CASSIUS
You are dense, Casca, and you either lack
Those sparks of life that should be in a Roman
Or do not use them. You look pale, and gaze,
And act afraid, and make yourself seem stunned   60
To see this strange displeasure in the heavens.
But if you would consider the true cause
For all these fires, for all these gliding ghosts,
Why birds and beasts act out of character,
Why old men, fools, and children see so well,   65
Why all these things veer from their natural function,
Their natures, their innate abilities
Toward deviant behavior, then you'll find
That Heaven has infused these things with powers
That make them instruments of fear and warn   70
Of greater deviance to come.
Now Casca, I could name for you the man
Most like this dreadful night, who thunders,
Who flashes lightening, opens graves, and roars,
Just like that lion in the Capitol,   75
A man no mightier than yourself or me
In aptitude, yet one who's grown as monstrous
And awful as these strange disturbances.

CASCA
It's Caesar that you mean, is it not, Cassius?

CASSIUS
Don't bother yet with who. For Romans now   80
Have meat and bones much like their ancestors.
But—these poor times—our fathers' minds are dead,

And we are governed by our mothers' spirits.
Submitting to this yoke is womanish.

CASCA
Indeed they say the senators tomorrow   85
Plan to establish Caesar as a king
Who'll wear his crown across all seas and lands,
In every place except in Italy.

CASSIUS
I know where I will wear this dagger then;
From bondage Cassius will deliver Cassius.   90
Through this, you gods, you make the weakest strong;
Through this, you gods, a tyrant you defeat.
No tower of stone, no walls of hammered brass,
No airless dungeon, no strong links of iron
Can ever hold the strength of spirit in,   95
But weary of these worldly barriers,
Life never lacks the power to free itself.
If I know this, then all the world should know,
The part of tyranny that I must bear
I can shake off at will.

[Thunder continues]

CASCA
                    And so can I,   100
So every slave then holds in his own hands
The power to cancel his captivity.

CASSIUS
Would Caesar wish to be a tyrant then?
Poor man, I know he won't become a wolf
Unless he sees us Romans act like sheep;   105
He'd be no lion, if Romans were not deer.
Those in a rush to make a mighty fire
Begin it with thin straws. What is Rome now?
Just twigs, just kindling, prunings when it serves
As the debris that's used to set on fire   110
So low a thing as Caesar! But, O grief,

Where have you led me? If I'm saying this
To Caesar's willing slave, I know that I
Must answer for these words, but I am armed,
And dangers aren't important to me now.   115

CASCA
It's Casca you are speaking to and not
Some sneering tattletale. Here, shake my hand.
If you will form a faction to redress
These grievances, then I will step as far
As he who goes the farthest.

CASSIUS
                    Then you're in.   120
Now I can tell you, Casca, I've already
Convinced a number of our noblest Romans
To undertake with me an enterprise
Of honorably dangerous consequence.
By now they're waiting in the colonnade   125
By Pompey's theatre.⁸ On a fearful night,
Like this, there's no one walking in the streets
And the condition of the skies above
Reminds us of the work that lies ahead,
Quite bloody, fiery, and quite terrible.   130

CASCA
Keep still a minute. Someone's rushing toward us.

CASSIUS
It's Cinna. I can tell by how he walks.
He is a friend.—

                    [Enter CINNA]

                    Cinna, why are you rushing?

CINNA (a patrician)
To find you. Who is that? Metellus Cimber?

CASSIUS
No, it is Casca, one aligned with us   135
In our endeavor. Are they waiting, Cinna?

CINNA
I am glad to hear it. What a fearful night!
There's two or three of us who've seen strange sights.

CASSIUS
Are they still waiting? Tell me.

CINNA
They are. O Cassius, if only you   140
Could win the noble Brutus to our side—

CASSIUS
Don't panic. Now, good Cinna, take this paper
And place it somewhere—in the praetor's chair—
Where only Brutus sees it. This one, throw
It through his window. This one, paste it on   145
The statue of old Brutus. When you're done,
Rejoin us at the colonnade at Pompey's.
Are Decius Brutus and Trebonius there?

CINNA
All but Metellus Cimber. He went off
To find you at your house. Now I'll get going   150
And put these papers where you told me to.

CASSIUS
When done, head back to Pompey's theatre.

[Exit CINNA]

Come, Casca, we must speak with Brutus at
His house before it's light. Three-fourths of him
We have already, and the rest of him   155
Should yield to us upon the next encounter.

CASCA
O, he's held high in all the people's hearts!
And what seems criminal in us becomes
With his support, as if through wizardry,
An act that's virtuous and honorable.   160

CASSIUS
Him, and his worth, and our great need for him,
You've illustrated vividly. Let's go.
It's after midnight, and before the dawn,
We'll wake him up and make sure he is with us.

[Exit]

Julius Caesar

Brutus

Act Two

Act Two

Scene One. Rome. Brutus' Garden

[Enter BRUTUS]

BRUTUS
Please, Lucius, come here!—
The stars are still too few for me to guess
How close it is to dawn.—Lucius, please!—
I wish I could be blamed for such sound sleeping.
Please, Lucius, please! Wake up, I say! Please, Lucius!   5

[Enter LUCIUS]

LUCIUS (servant of Brutus)
You called, my lord?

BRUTUS
I need a candle in my study, Lucius.
When it is lit, come back out here and get me.

LUCIUS
I will, my lord.

[Exit LUCIUS]

BRUTUS
It means that he must die. I cannot find   10
A personal complaint to kick him with,
Just public ones. He wishes to be crowned.
How that might change his nature, that's the question.
It's sunny days that bring the adder out,
And that means watchful walking. Crown him king?   15

Yes, I agree, we're giving him the fangs
With which to cause great harm if he so chooses.
Abuse of greatness comes when mercy is
Divorced from power. True, I've never seen
Emotions ruling Caesar anymore   20
Than reason would. But often it's the case
That humbleness is young ambition's ladder,
Towards which he turns his face as he ascends,
But just as he attains the highest step,
He turns so that the ladder's at his back,   25
Looks in the clouds, scorning the lower rungs
That he has scaled. And Caesar may do this
Unless forestalled. But since the facts cannot
Be colored to support a case against him,
We'll argue this: an augmentation of   30
His power would lead to this or that excess,
So we must see him as a serpent's egg—
A harmful thing by nature if it's hatched—
And kill him in the shell.

[Re-enter LUCIUS]

LUCIUS
The candle's burning in your study, sir.   35
Searching the windowsill for flint, I found
This folded piece of paper, and I am sure
It wasn't there before I went to bed.

BRUTUS
Go back to bed, boy. It's not morning yet.
Tomorrow, isn't it the ides of March?   40

LUCIUS
I don't know, sir.

BRUTUS
Go check the calendar, and bring me word.

LUCIUS
I will, sir.

[Exit LUCIUS]

BRUTUS
The shooting stars now whizzing in the air
Give so much light that I can read by them.   45

[Opens the letter and reads]

"Brutus, you're sleeping. Awake and see yourself.
Will Rome...you know this. Speak, strike, rectify!
Brutus, you are asleep. Wake up!"
Such calls to action often have been dropped
Where I have picked them up.   50
"Will Rome...you know this." So I must fill these blanks.
Will Rome endure a single ruler? What, Rome?
My ancestors expelled Tarquinius from[1]
The streets of Rome when he was called a king.
"Speak, strike, and rectify!"—Is this my call   55
To speak and strike? O Rome, I promise you,
If things are rectified, you will receive
All that you asked for from the hand of Brutus!

[Re-enter LUCIUS]

LUCIUS
Sir, March has used up fifteen days.

[Knocking is heard]

BRUTUS
That's fine. Go to the gate. Somebody's knocking.   60

[Exit LUCIUS]

Since Cassius first honed my opposition,
I have not slept.
Between the doing of a dreadful thing
And the first impulse, that whole interval
Is like a phantom or a hideous dream.   65
Our guardian spirit and our human powers
Are in debate, and like a little kingdom,

The state that is a man then suffers from
A kind of insurrection.

[Re-enter LUCIUS]

LUCIUS
Sir, it's your brother-in-law Cassius,   70
And he desires to see you.

BRUTUS
                              Is he alone?

LUCIUS
No, sir, there are more with him.

BRUTUS
                              Do you know them?

LUCIUS
No, sir, their hats are pulled down to their ears,
With half their faces buried in their robes.
There isn't any way to recognize them   75
From any of their features.

BRUTUS
                              Let 'em enter.

[Exit LUCIUS]

It is the faction.—O conspiracy,
Aren't you ashamed to show your dangerous brow
By night when evil runs most free? Where will
You find a cavern dark enough by day   80
To mask your monstrous face? You won't, conspiracy.
Hide it in smiles and affability,
For if you roam around without disguise,
The path to hell will not be dim enough
To hide you from detection.   85

[Enter CASSIUS, CASCA, DECIUS, CINNA, METEL-
LUS Cimber, and TREBONIUS]

CASSIUS
I think our bold assault's disturbed your rest.
Good morning, Brutus. Are we bothering you?

BRUTUS
I'm still up at this hour, awake all night.
Do I know all these men who came with you?

CASSIUS
Yes, every one of them. There's no man here   90
Who doesn't honor you, and they all wish
You held the same opinion of yourself
That every noble Roman also shares.
This is Trebonius.

BRUTUS
                          He is welcome here.

CASSIUS
This Decius Brutus.

BRUTUS
                          He is welcome too.   95

CASSIUS
Here's Casca, here's Cinna, and here's Metellus Cimber.

BRUTUS
They are all welcome.
What worrisome cares have interposed themselves
Between your eyes and sleep?

CASSIUS
May we speak privately?   100

            [BRUTUS and CASSIUS step aside to whisper]

DECIUS (a patrician)
This way is east. The day should break here, right?

CASCA
No.

CINNA
I'm sorry, sir, it does and those grey lines
That lace the clouds are messengers of day.

CASCA
You'll soon admit that you are both mistaken.   105
Here, where I point my sword, the sun is rising
And rapidly advancing from the south,
No doubt because we're early in the year.
Two months from now or so, more toward the north
He first displays his fire. Due east is there,   110
Exactly where the Capitol is standing.

[BRUTUS and CASSIUS rejoin the others]

BRUTUS
Give me your hands, all of you, one by one.

CASSIUS
And let us swear to our determination.

BRUTUS
No, not an oath. The faces of these men,
The suffering of our souls, and this abuse—   115
If motives such as these are weak, then let's
Break off at once and lounge around in bed.
We'll let high-flying tyranny roam wide,
Till chance takes each man down. But if this cause,
As I am sure it does, holds heat enough   120
To kindle cowards and to steel with valor
The melting spirits of women, then, countrymen,
What other spur beyond our cause could prod
Us on to set this right? What other bond
Beyond a Roman's confidential pledge   125
To play no tricks? What other oath beyond
What honest men have promised honest men—
That this shall come to be or we will die?
Let priests and cowards swear, the overcautious,
Old feeble corpses, and those suffering types   130
Who welcome wrongs. It's to bad causes that

Such dubious creatures swear. But do not stain
The steadfast virtue of our enterprise
Nor our indomitable strength of spirit
By thinking that our cause or undertaking   135
Requires an oath—when every drop of blood
That every Roman bears, and nobly bears,
Will each be shown to be a bastard's blood
If he should break the smallest particle
Of any promise that has come from him.   140

CASSIUS
But how 'bout Cicero? Shall we sound him out?
I think he'll stand behind us very strongly.

CASCA
Don't let us leave him out.

CINNA
                                No, by no means.

METELLUS (a patrician)
Let's bring him in and use his silver hair
To purchase good opinions of us all   145
And buy men's voices to commend our deeds.
It will be said his judgment guides our hand.
Our youth and wildness won't stand out at all
But will be buried in his dignity.

BRUTUS
No, not that name! We'd best not bring him in,   150
For he will never follow any thing
That other men began.

CASSIUS
Then leave him out.

CASCA
                                Indeed, he won't fit in.

DECIUS
Will Caesar be the only one we touch?

CASSIUS
Decius, good point.—It isn't fitting that   155
Mark Antony, who so admires Caesar,
Should outlive Caesar. We shall find in him
A dangerous schemer, with the means, you know,
Should he make use of them, to reach out far
And hurt us all. If we are to prevent this,   160
Caesar and Antony must fall together.

BRUTUS
Our deeds will seem too bloody, Caius Cassius,
If we cut off the head, then hack the limbs—
Like death from rage, with malice following—
For Antony is just a limb of Caesar.   165
Let's sacrifice, but not be butchers, Caius.
We're standing up against the spirit of Caesar,
And in the spirit of men there is no blood.
If only we could get at Caesar's spirit
Without dismembering Caesar! But, alas,   170
Caesar must bleed for it! So, noble friends,
Let's kill him boldly, but not wrathfully.
Let's carve from him a dish fit for the gods,
Not hack from him a carcass fit for hounds.
And let our hearts, as clever masters do,   175
Provoke their servants to act out of rage,
And then pretend to scold them. This will make
Our deeds seem necessary, not malicious;
Appearing thus, those in the public eye,
Will call us surgeons, and not murderers.[2]   180
As for Mark Antony, don't dwell on him,
For he can't hurt us more than Caesar's arm
Once Caesar's head is off.

CASSIUS
                              Yet I still fear him.
He has a deeply grafted love for Caesar.

BRUTUS
Good Cassius, please, don't let him worry you.   185
If he loves Caesar, all that he can do

Is harm himself—just brood and die for Caesar.
And that is not like him, for he is drawn
To sports, to wildness, and likes company.

TREBONIUS (a patrician)
He is no threat. He doesn't need to die,   190
For he will live and laugh when this is over.

[Clock strikes][3]

BRUTUS
Hush. Count the time.

CASSIUS
                    The clock has struck three times.

TREBONIUS
It's time to part.

CASSIUS
                    But we are still not sure
If Caesar will appear today or not,
For lately he's been growing superstitious,   195
Quite different from the strong views he once held
Of fantasies, of dreams, and prophecies.
It may be that the sight of all these wonders,
The unaccustomed terror of this night,
And all this talk of omens from his priests   200
Will keep him from the Capitol today.

DECIUS
No chance. If that's what he's resolved to do,
I'll change his mind. He loves to hear how horns
Of charging unicorns can be betrayed
By trees, and bears by mirrors, and lions by nets,   205
And elephants by pits, and men by flattery.
But when I tell him he hates flatterers,
He says he does, and then is flattered most.
I'll work on him.
For I know how to turn his mood around   210
And get him over to the Capitol.

CASSIUS
No, all of us will be there to escort him.

BRUTUS
By eight o'clock. Is that the very latest?

CINNA
The very latest. And you must be there.

METELLUS
Caius Ligarius built up quite a grudge   215
When Caesar scolded him for praising Pompey.
I wonder why you haven't thought of him.

BRUTUS
Then, good Metellus, see him on the way.
He's close to me, and he knows all our thinking.
Just send him here, and I'll get him to join.   220

CASSIUS
The morning has arrived. We'll leave you, Brutus.
And, friends, disperse, but all of you remember
What you have said, and show that you're true Romans.

BRUTUS
Good gentlemen, look bright and merry now.
We shouldn't wear our plans upon our face   225
But pull this off like Roman actors do,
With tireless energy and dignity.
And so, good morning to each one of you.

[Exit all but BRUTUS]

Boy! Lucius!—Fast asleep? It does not matter.
Enjoy the honey-heavy dew of slumber.   230
You lack the fictions and the fantasies,
Which restlessness draws in the brains of men.
That's why you sleep so sound.

[Enter PORTIA]

PORTIA (wife of Brutus)
> Brutus, my lord!

BRUTUS
Portia, what is it? Why are you awake?
It isn't healthy for you to expose   235
Your weak condition to the raw, cold morning.

Lucius

PORTIA
It harms you too. You slipped unkindly, Brutus
Out of my bed. And last night, during supper,
You suddenly arose, and walked around,
Fretting and sighing, with your two arms crossed,   240
And when I asked you what the matter was,
You stared straight at me with an unkind look.
I asked again, but then you scratched your head
And quite infuriated stamped your foot.
When I insisted, still you would not answer,   245
But with an angry gesture with your hand,

You signaled I should leave. And so I did,
Afraid I'd strengthen an infuriation
Already too inflamed and hopeful that
It was no more than just some passing mood,   250
Which sometimes spends an hour in every man.
It will not let you eat, or talk, or sleep,
And if this thing could alter your appearance
As much as it's transformed your disposition,
I would not recognize you. My dear lord,   255
Acquaint me with the cause of all your grief.

BRUTUS
I am not feeling well, and that is all.

PORTIA
Brutus is wise, and, if his health were poor,
He'd welcome any means that made him well.

BRUTUS
And so I do. Good Portia, go to bed.   260

PORTIA
Is Brutus sick? And is it common practice
To go outside half-dressed and breathe the vapors
Of a damp morning? What, is Brutus sick
And yet will sneak out of his wholesome bed
To risk the vile contagion of the night,   265
And tempt the dank, contaminated air
To add on to his sickness? No, my Brutus,
You have some sick disorder in your mind,
Which, owing to my standing as your wife,
I ought to recognize. [kneels] Upon my knees,   270
I beg you, by my once commended beauty,
By all your vows of love and that great vow
Which joined us and has made us into one—
Reveal to me, yourself, your other half,
Why you're so solemn, and what men tonight   275
Have paid a visit here, for there have been
Some six or seven, with their faces shaded
Despite the darkness.

BRUTUS
                    Do not kneel, kind Portia.

PORTIA
I'd have no need, if you were kind, my husband.
Are there, within the bonds of marriage, Brutus,   280
Exceptions that restrict what I may know
Of secrets that you keep? I'm one with you
But held to time and manner limitations—
To share your meals, add comfort to your bed,
And sometimes talk ? Am I lodged at the edge of town,   285
Kept for your pleasure? If that's all I am,
Portia is Brutus' harlot, not his wife.

BRUTUS
You are my true and honorable wife,
As dear to me as are the rosy drops
That visit my sad heart.   290

PORTIA
If this were true, then I should know this secret.
I grant I am a woman—furthermore,
A woman that Lord Brutus made his wife.
I grant I am a woman—furthermore,
A woman well respected, Cato's daughter.[4]   295
Do you think I'm no stronger than my sex,
With such a father and with such a husband?
Include me in your plans. I won't disclose them.
I've shown to you strong proof of my resolve—
A voluntary wound I gave myself   300
Here in my thigh. Could I endure that calmly
And yet not keep your secrets?

BRUTUS
                    O you gods,
Render me worthy of this noble wife!

                    [Knocking is heard]

Hear that, there's knocking. Portia, wait inside,

And soon enough your bosom too will hold   305
The secrets of my heart.
All this activity I will explain
And all the sadness squeezed into my brow.
Leave quickly.

[Exit PORTIA]

—Lucius, who is that knocking?

[Re-enter LUCIUS with LIGARIUS]

LUCIUS
An ailing man who hopes to speak with you.   310

BRUTUS
It's Caius Ligarius, whom Metellus spoke of.—
Aside, boy.

[LUCIUS exits]

—Caius Ligarius, what's all this?

LIGARIUS (a patrician)
Accept "Good day", please, from a feeble tongue.

BRUTUS
O, what a time you've chosen, noble Caius,
To need a scarf! I wish you were not sick!   315

LIGARIUS
I'll be well soon if Brutus has in hand
A mission worthy of the name of honor.

BRUTUS
And such a thing I have in hand, Ligarius,
If your two ears are well enough to hear it.

LIGARIUS
By all the gods that Romans bow before,   320

I now discard my sickness. Soul of Rome!
Brave son, derived from honorable loins!
You, like a sorcerer, have conjured up
My deadened spirit. Order me to run,
I'll strive against what is impossible—   325
I'll get the better of it. What's the plan?

BRUTUS
A piece of work to make the sick feel well.

LIGARIUS
But aren't we here to make some well ones sick?

BRUTUS
That's also part of this. What it is, Caius,
I will reveal to you as we head toward   330
The one to whom it must be done.

LIGARIUS
                                                Proceed,
And with a fired up heart I'll follow you,
To do I know not what, but it's enough
If Brutus leads the way.

BRUTUS
                                        Follow me then.

                                    [Exit]

Scene Two. Caesar's House

                    [Thunder and lightning]
            [Enter JULIUS CAESAR, in his dressing gown]

JULIUS CAESAR
Both heaven and earth are not at peace tonight.
Three times Calpurnia's cried out in her sleep,
"Help, ho! They're murdering Caesar!"—Who's on duty?

[Enter a SERVANT]

SERVANT
My lord?

JULIUS CAESAR
Go tell the priests to start the sacrifice,   5
And bring me their results immediately.

SERVANT
I will, my lord.

[Exit]
[Enter CALPURNIA]

CALPURNIA (Caesar's wife)
What is this, Caesar? Are you going out?
You really shouldn't leave the house today.

JULIUS CAESAR
Caesar shall go. The things that threaten me   10
Have only seen my back. Once they can see
The face of Caesar, they will disappear.

CALPURNIA
Caesar, I've never paid much heed to omens,
Yet now they frighten me. Besides these things
We've heard and seen, there's someone here who's now   15
Recounting horrid sights the night watch saw.
A lioness was whelping in the streets;
And graves gaped open, yielding up their dead;
Fierce fiery warriors fought upon the clouds
In ranks and squares and proper battle order   20
And drizzled blood upon the Capitol.
The noise of battle hurtled through the air,
The horses neighed, the dying soldiers groaned
And shrieking ghosts were squealing on the streets.
O Caesar, none of these are normal things,   25
And I do fear them!

JULIUS CAESAR
How can we avoid
An outcome that the mighty gods intend?
So Caesar will go out, for these predictions
Apply to all the world, not only Caesar.

CALPURNIA
When beggars die, no comets will be seen.   30
The sky ignites upon the death of princes.

JULIUS CAESAR
Cowards die many times before their deaths;
The valiant never taste of death but once.
Of all the wonders that I've ever seen,
It seems to me so strange that men fear death,   35
Given that death is inescapable
And comes when it will come.—

[Re-enter SERVANT]

The priests' report?

SERVANT
They say you'd best not venture out today.
They plucked the entrails from the sacrifice
And could not find a heart within the beast.   40

JULIUS CAESAR
The gods do this to bring a coward shame.
Caesar's indeed a beast without a heart
If he stays home today because of fear.
No, Caesar shall not. Danger is my twin
And knows full well that I'm the dangerous one.   45
We are two lions born on the same day,
And I'm the elder and more terrible.
And Caesar shall go out.

CALPURNIA
I worry, lord,
Your wisdom's been consumed by confidence.

Do not go out today. Say it's my fear   50
That keeps you in the house and not your own.
We'll send Mark Antony to the Senate House,
And have him say that you're not well today.
Let me, down on my knee, prevail in this.

[CALPURNIA kneels]

JULIUS CAESAR
Mark Antony will say that I'm not well.   55
To satisfy this whim, I will stay home.

[Enter DECIUS]

Here's Decius Brutus. He will tell them that.

[CALPURNIA rises]

DECIUS
Caesar, all hail! Good morning, worthy Caesar
I've come to take you to the Senate House.

JULIUS CAESAR
And you have come here at the perfect time   60
To send my greetings to the senators
And tell them that I will not come today.
"Cannot" is false and " dare not" even falser.
I will not come today. Tell them that, Decius.

CALPURNIA
Say he is sick.

JULIUS CAESAR
                 Should Caesar send a lie?   65
Have I in conquest stretched my reach so far
That I fear telling greybeard men the truth?—
Decius, go tell them Caesar will not come.

DECIUS
Most mighty Caesar, let me know the cause,
Or I'll be laughed at when I tell them that.   70

JULIUS CAESAR
The cause—it is my will. I will not come.
That is enough to satisfy the Senate.
To satisfy your personal concern,
Because you're dear to me, I'll let you know.
Calpurnia, my wife, wants me at home.   75
She saw my statue in a dream last night,
Which, like a fountain with a hundred spouts,
Ran with pure blood; and many joyous Romans
Were smiling there and washed their hands in it.
And this she sees as warnings and as threats   80
Of evils imminent, and on her knee
She begged that I not leave the house today.

DECIUS
This dream has been interpreted all wrong.
It was a sign of better things to come.
Your statue spouting blood from many pipes   85
In which so many smiling Romans bathed
Must show us that great Rome will suck from you
Reviving blood and that great men will strive
To stain their garments and insignia with it.[5]
Calpurnia's dream is signifying this.   90

JULIUS CAESAR
In this way, you've explained it very well.

DECIUS
Especially when you hear what else I have.
I'll tell you now: the Senate has decided
To give a crown today to mighty Caesar.
So if you send them word you will not come,   95
Their minds may change. And then someone is apt
To make a joke of it and likely say
"The Senate is in recess till a time
When Caesar's wife is blessed with better dreams."
If Caesar hides himself, then won't they whisper   100
"Look, Caesar is afraid?"
Pardon me, Caesar, but because I love
To see you prosper, I must tell you this.
Propriety is overruled by love.

JULIUS CAESAR
How foolish all your fears seem now, Calpurnia!   105
I am ashamed that I gave in to them.
Give me my robe, for I will go.

[Enter PUBLIUS, BRUTUS, LIGARIUS, METELLUS,
CASCA, TREBONIUS, and CINNA]

And Publius has come here to escort me.

PUBLIUS (a senator)
Good morning, Caesar.

JULIUS CAESAR
              Welcome, Publius.—
Ah, Brutus, are you up so early too?—   110
Good morning, Casca.—Caius Ligarius,
Caesar was not as bad an enemy
As is this fever which has made you lean.—
What is the time?

BRUTUS
              Caesar, it now is eight.

JULIUS CAESAR
I thank you for your pains and courtesy.   115

[Enter MARK ANTONY]

Look! Antony, carousing all night long,
Yet up in spite of that.—Good morning, Antony.

MARK ANTONY
The same most noble Caesar.

JULIUS CAESAR
              [to CALPURNIA] Have them
prepare some wine.

[CALPURNIA exits]

I am the one to blame for this delay.—
Ah, Cinna—Ah, Metellus—What, Trebonius!   120
I've put aside an hour to talk with you.
Don't forget to call on me today.
Stay near me so that I'll remember it.

TREBONIUS
Caesar, I will. [Aside] And so near will I be,
That your best friends will wish I had been further.   125

JULIUS CAESAR
Good friends, go in, and taste some wine with me.
And we, like friends, we'll go on in together.

BRUTUS
[Aside] But, Caesar, "like" is not the same as "being."
To think about it grieves the heart of Brutus!

[Exit all]

Scene Three. A Street Near the Capitol

[Enter ARTEMIDORUS, reading a document]

ARTEMIDORUS (a teacher of rhetoric)
[reads] "Caesar, beware of Brutus, take heed of Cassius,
don't come near Casca, keep an eye on Cinna, don't trust
Trebonius, watch closely Metellus Cimber, Decius Brutus
has no love for you, you have wronged Caius Ligarius. All
these men are of just one mind, and it has turned against   5
Caesar. If you are not immortal, watch what you do. Over-
confidence clears a path for conspiracy. May the mighty
gods defend you!

Your devoted friend, Artemidorus."

I'll stand right here till Caesar passes by   10

And give him this like some petitioner.
My heart laments that virtue cannot live
Far from the teeth of those who envy it.
O Caesar read this. Then you might survive.
If not, then gods and traitors will connive.   15

[Exit]

Scene Four. Outside Brutus' House

[Enter PORTIA and LUCIUS]

PORTIA
I beg you, boy, run to the Senate-house.
Don't wait to find out why. Get going now.
Why are you waiting?

LUCIUS
                         To run what errand, madam?

PORTIA
I could have had you there and back again
In less time than it takes to tell you why.   5
[Aside] O, fortitude, be strongly on my side!
Put a huge mountain 'tween my heart and tongue!
I have a man's mind, but a woman's strength.
How hard it is for women to keep secrets!—
Are you still here?

LUCIUS
                         Madam, what should I do?   10
Run to the Capitol, and nothing else?
And then return to you, and nothing else?

PORTIA
Yes, go and see, boy, if your lord looks well.
He looked sick when he left. Watch carefully

What Caesar does and who petitions him.   15
Boy, listen! What's that noise?

LUCIUS

There's nothing, madam.

PORTIA
Just listen please.
I heard a frantic outcry, like a fight,
And the wind brings it from the Capitol.

LUCIUS
Truly, mam, I hear nothing.   20

[Enter SOOTHSAYER]

PORTIA
You, fellow. Where were you just coming from?

SOOTHSAYER
From my own house, good lady.

PORTIA
What time is it?

SOOTHSAYER
It's nine o'clock or so.

PORTIA
Has Caesar gone yet to the Capitol?

SOOTHSAYER
Madam, not yet. I'm heading for a spot   25
Where I can see him as he passes by.

PORTIA
Do you intend to give him some petition?

SOOTHSAYER
Lady, I do. If Caesar's kind enough
To do himself a favor and to listen,
I'll beg him to be friendly to himself.   30

PORTIA
Is there some harm that is intended towards him?

SOOTHSAYER
None that I know for sure, but much I fear may happen.
Good morning to you.—Here the street is narrow.
That throng at Caesar's heels, of senators,
Of judges, citizens with their petitions,   35
Will almost crowd a feeble man to death.
I'll find an emptier place and there I'll try
To speak to Caesar as he comes along.

[Exit SOOTHSAYER]

PORTIA
I must go in.—[Aside] Oh my, how weak a thing
The heart of woman is!—O Brutus,   45
Let's hope your enterprise has heaven's help!—
What if the boy heard?—[to LUCIUS] Brutus' petition—
No, Caesar will not grant it. [Aside]—O, I feel faint.—
[to LUCIUS] Run, Lucius, run. Give my lord my regards.
Say that my spirit's fine and then come back.   50
And bring me word of what he says to you.

[Exit in different directions]

Julius Caesar

Caesar and Calpurnia

Act Three

Act Three

Scene One. Rome. In Front of the Capitol

[A crowd of people in the street leading into the Capitol,
among them ARTEMIDORUS and the SOOTHSAYER.
The SENATORS are seated inside. Flourish. Enter JU-
LIUS CAESAR, BRUTUS, CASSIUS, CASCA, DECIUS,
METELLUS, TREBONIUS, CINNA, MARK ANTONY,
LEPIDUS, POPILIUS Lena, PUBLIUS, and others]

JULIUS CAESAR
The ides of March have come.

SOOTHSAYER
Yes, Caesar, but not over.

ARTEMIDORUS
Hail, Caesar! Read this note.

DECIUS
Trebonius is hoping you'll read first,
When you have time, his humble document.   5

ARTEMIDORUS
O Caesar, read mine first, for mine will touch
Great Caesar personally. Read it, Caesar.

JULIUS CAESAR
What touches closest must be dealt with last.

ARTEMIDORUS
You can't wait, Caesar. Read it right away.

JULIUS CAESAR
What, is the fellow mad?

PUBLIUS

        Sir, step aside.   10

CASSIUS
What's this? Petition Caesar in the street?
Come to the Capitol.

[JULIUS CAESAR enters the Capitol, the rest following.
        All the SENATORS rise]

POPILIUS (a senator)
I hope your enterprise today succeeds.

CASSIUS
What enterprise, Popilius?

POPILIUS

        Fare you well.

[POPILIUS moves to join Caesar]

BRUTUS
What did Popilius Lena say?   15

CASSIUS
He hopes our enterprise today succeeds.
I fear now that our plan has been revealed.

BRUTUS
Look, how he moves toward Caesar. Watch him.

CASSIUS
Casca, move quickly. We're afraid they'll stop us.—
Brutus, what should we do? If we're exposed,   20
We can't turn back. It's Cassius or it's Caesar,
For I will slay myself.

BRUTUS
        Keep steady, Cassius.
Popilius Lena has not spoiled our plan.
Look there, he's smiling. Caesar has not changed.

CASSIUS
Trebonius knows his cue. There, Brutus, look.   25
He's drawn Mark Antony out of the way.

[Exit MARK ANTONY and TREBONIUS]

DECIUS
Where is Metellus Cimber? Now is when
He must present to Caesar his petition.

BRUTUS
He's ready now. Move close. Give him support.

CINNA
Casca, you'll be the first to lift your hand.   30

JULIUS CAESAR
Are we all ready? Is there something wrong
That Caesar and his Senate must correct?

METELLUS
Most high, most mighty, and most potent Caesar,
Metellus Cimber throws in front of you
His humble heart.

[Kneeling]

JULIUS CAESAR
                    I must restrain you, Cimber.   35
This genuflection and deep curtsying
Might stir the blood of common men and make
Our pre-ordained and settled laws seem like
The rules of children's games.¹ It's foolishness
To think that Caesar's blood rebels so much   40
That its true nature will be thawed away
By that which melts a fool's—I mean, sweet words,
And deep-bent knees, and fawning like a spaniel.
Your brother has been banished by decree.
If you bow down and pray and fawn for him,   45
I'll kick you like a mutt out of my way.
Caesar was not unjust. Without good cause,
There can be no appeal.

METELLUS
Is there no voice more worthy than my own,
To state more sweetly in great Caesar's ear   50
The case against the exile of my brother?

BRUTUS
I'll kiss your hand, and not to flatter Caesar,
But to request that Publius Cimber be
Immediately recalled from banishment.

JULIUS CAESAR
What, Brutus?

CASSIUS
          [kneeling] Forgive me, Caesar. Forgive me.   55
As low as your two feet will Cassius kneel
To beg that you restore his former status.

JULIUS CAESAR
I'd easily be moved, were I like you.
My pleas move you; your pleas would then move me.
But I'm as constant as the northern star,   60
Its point so fixed, its quality so lasting
That there's no equal in the firmament.
The skies are painted with uncounted sparks,
They all are made of fire, and each one shines,
But of them all, just one remains in place.   65
Our world's the same: it is well-stocked with men,
And men are flesh and blood, and comprehending;
Yet of that number I know of just one
Who resolutely keeps hold of his rank,
Unstirred by other movements. I'm that man,   70
As I have shown you on this minor point
Where I was firm that Cimber should be banished,
And firm I will remain to keep him so.

          [CINNA moves forward and kneels]

CINNA
O Caesar—

JULIUS CAESAR
          Go! You wish to lift Olympus?

DECIUS
Great Caesar—

JULIUS CAESAR
       Even Brutus kneels in vain!   75

CASCA
These hands speak for me!

[CASCA, BRUTUS, and the conspirators stab CAESAR]

JULIUS CAESAR
Et tu, Brute?[2] —Then let Caesar fall.

       [JULIUS CAESAR dies]

CINNA
Liberty! Freedom! Tyranny is dead!—
Run out, proclaim it, yell it in the streets.

CASSIUS
Go climb the public platforms and cry out,   80
"Liberty, freedom, banishment no more!"

BRUTUS
People and senators, don't be alarmed,
Don't flee, stay calm. Ambition's paid its debt.

CASCA
Go to the platform, Brutus.

DECIUS
       And Cassius too.

BRUTUS
Where's Publius?   85

CINNA
He's here, quite overwhelmed by all this uproar.

METELLUS
Stay close together, lest some friend of Caesar's
Should happen to—

BRUTUS
No need for that.—Don't worry, Publius!
No one intends to do harm to your person   90
Nor any other Roman. Tell them, Publius.

CASSIUS
And leave now, Publius, in case the people
Rush up at us. Your age puts you in danger.

BRUTUS
Yes, do—and no man should pay for this deed
But we the doers.   95

[Non-conspirators leave. Enter TREBONIUS]

CASSIUS
Where's Antony?

TREBONIUS
            He fled home stupefied.
Men, wives, and children gape, cry out, and run,
As if it's doomsday.

BRUTUS
            Fate, in time we'll know

Your will. We know we'll die; it's just the time
And how the days draw out that men dispute.   100

CASCA
Whoever cuts off twenty years of life
Cuts off that many years of fearing death.

BRUTUS
Agree to that, then death's a benefit.
That makes us Caesar's friends, since we've reduced
His time of fearing death.—Stoop, Romans, stoop,   105
And let us bathe our hands in Caesar's blood
Up to the elbows, smear our swords with it,
And then go forth—yes, to the Forum there,
And waving our red weapons o'er our heads,
Let's all cry, "Peace, freedom, and liberty!"   110

CASSIUS
Then bend and wash. How many ages hence
Will this majestic scene be reenacted
In states unborn and tongues yet to be heard!

BRUTUS
How often on the stage will Caesar bleed,
Stretched out along the base of Pompey's statue,   115
No worthier than dust!

CASSIUS
                    As often as that is,
This band shall just as often hear us called
The men who gave their country liberty.

DECIUS
Should we go out?

CASSIUS
                    Yes, every man will come.
Brutus shall lead, and we'll be at his heels   120
Among the boldest and best hearts of Rome.

BRUTUS
Hold on, who's this?

[Enter a SERVANT]

A friend of Antony's.

SERVANT
My master, Brutus, said to kneel like this.
Mark Antony told me I should fall down,
And, when I'm prostrate, I should tell you this: 125
Brutus is noble, wise, valiant, and honest;
Caesar was mighty, bold, princely, and loving.
Say I love Brutus and I honor him;
Say I feared Caesar, honored him, and loved him.
If Brutus will permit Mark Antony   130
To safely come to him and be assured
That Caesar does deserve to lie here dead,
Then Antony shall not love Caesar dead
As much as Brutus living, but will follow
The fortunes and affairs of noble Brutus   135
Through all the hazards on this untried path
With full support. So says my master Antony.

BRUTUS
Your master is a wise and valiant Roman.
I've never thought him less.
Tell him to come here if that is his wish,   140
To satisfy himself, and, on my honor,
Depart untouched.

SERVANT
                          I'll bring him here at once.

[Exit]

BRUTUS
I know that we can count him as a friend.

CASSIUS
I hope we can, but I still have a mind
That fears him greatly; usually my suspicions   145
Are deadly accurate.

BRUTUS
Shhh. Here comes Antony.—

[Enter MARK ANTONY]

Welcome, Mark Antony.

MARK ANTONY
O mighty Caesar! Do you lie so low?
Have all your conquests, glories, triumphs, gains,
Shrunk down to this small parcel? Fare thee well.—   150
I don't know what you gentlemen intend,
Who else you'll bleed, who else will swell and rot.
If I am one, no hour fits as well
As Caesar's death-hour, and no instrument
Is half as worthy as these swords made rich   155
With the most noble blood in all this world.
I plead with you, if you bear me a grudge,
Now, while your purple hands still fume and steam,
Fulfill your wish. If I live to one thousand,
I'll never find myself more primed to die,   160
No place, no means of death would please me more
Than to be here by Caesar, cut by you,
The best, most worthy spirits of our age.

BRUTUS
O Antony, don't ask us for your death!
Though we must seem so bloody and so cruel—   165
No doubt our hands and our most recent deed
Suggest we are—you're seeing just our hands
And this, the bloody business they have done.
Our hearts you do not see; they're full of pity;
And pity for the general wrongs Rome suffers   170
Has driven out (as fire drives out fire)
What we may feel for Caesar. As for you,
Our swords have blunted points, Mark Antony.
With arms so strong when violent,[3] and hearts
Like those of brothers, we now welcome you   175
With kindness, love, good thoughts, and all respect.

CASSIUS
Your voice shall be as strong as any man's
In allocation of new offices.

BRUTUS
Till we've appeased the multitudes, be patient—
Right now they are besides themselves with fear—   180
And then we will report to you why I,
Who still felt love for Caesar when I struck him,
Would take this step.

MARK ANTONY
                              I do not doubt your wisdom.
Let each man here extend his bloody hand.
First, Marcus Brutus, I will shake with you.   185
Next, Caius Cassius, I will take your hand.
Now, Decius Brutus, yours; now yours, Metellus;
Yours, Cinna; and, my valiant Casca, yours;
Last, though not least in love, yours, good Trebonius.
Gentlemen all—oh my, what shall I say?   190
My reputation's on such slippery ground,
You must conceive of me in one of two
Bad ways—a coward or a flatterer.
That I did love you, Caesar, it is true!
If you are looking on us now, could death   195
Have caused your soul to feel a grief so sharp
As seeing Antony here making peace,
Shaking the bloody fingers of your foes—
Noble one—in the presence of your corpse?
Had I as many eyes as you have wounds,   200
Weeping as fast as this blood streaming forth,
I would be better suited than to be
On friendly terms here with your enemies.
Forgive me, brave one....A hart set on by hounds.
And here you fell, and here your hunters stand,   205
Stained by your slaughter, crimsoned by your flow.
O world, you were the forest this hart roamed,
And this, indeed, O world, became your heart.
And now you lie here like some deer struck down
By all these princes!   210

CASSIUS
Mark Antony—

MARK ANTONY
          Pardon me, Caius Cassius,
But Caesar's enemies should say all this,
For, in a friend, it's too composed and modest.

CASSIUS
I do not mind you praising Caesar so,
But do we have an understanding here?   215
Should we include you on our list of friends,
Or carry on and not depend on you?

MARK ANTONY
That's why I took your hands but was indeed
Distracted some when looking down on Caesar.
I'm friends with all of you, and love you all,   220
And truly hope you'll tell me how and why
It was that Caesar here was dangerous.

BRUTUS
If not, it's just a savage spectacle.
Our reasons are so carefully considered
That if you, Antony, were Caesar's son,   225
You would be satisfied.

MARK ANTONY
                    That's all I seek,
With just this one request to you that I
May take his body to the market-place,
And on the rostrum, as becomes a friend,
May speak at some point at his funeral.   230

BRUTUS
You shall, Mark Antony.

CASSIUS
                    Brutus, a word with you.
[Aside to BRUTUS] What do you think you're doing? You
    cannot let

Mark Antony speak at his funeral.
Just think how much the people could be moved
By all that he may say.

BRUTUS
[Aside to CASSIUS] With your approval   235
I'll go myself onto the rostrum first,
And give the reasons for our Caesar's death.
Whatever Antony may say, I'll claim
He says it with our leave and our consent,
And we agree that Caesar shall enjoy   240
All due and proper rites and ceremonies.
The gain to us will outweigh any wrongs.

CASSIUS
[Aside to Brutus] I don't know what will happen. I don't
   like it.

BRUTUS
Mark Antony, here, you take Caesar's body.
Your eulogy must not blame us but state   245
What qualities of Caesar come to mind
And tell them that you speak with our permission
Or else you will not have a hand at all
In his memorial. And you will speak
From the same rostrum where I'm going now   250
After my speech has ended.

MARK ANTONY
                              It's agreed.
I want no more than that.

BRUTUS
Prepare the body, then, and follow us.
            [Exit all but MARK ANTONY]

MARK ANTONY
Forgive me, please, you bleeding piece of earth,
For being meek and gentle with these butchers!   255
Here are the ruins of the noblest man
That ever glided on the tide of time.

O, curse the hands that shed this precious blood!
Over your wounds—these silent mouths that part
Their ruby lips and beg my tongue to voice   260
And utter this—I make this prophesy:
A curse shall fall upon the limbs of men.
Internal fury and fierce civil strife
Shall overwhelm all parts of Italy.
Blood and destruction shall be spread so wide   265
And dreadful sights will be so commonplace
That mothers merely smile when they behold
Their infants chopped up by the hands of war,
All pity choked when cruel deeds are routine.
And Caesar's spirit, roving for revenge,   270
Its goddess by his side hot out of Hell,
Shall from these confines with a monarch's voice
Cry "Havoc!" and unleash the dogs of war,
So this foul deed can smell above the earth
With rotting men, groaning for burial.   275

[Enter a SERVANT]

You serve Octavius Caesar, do you not?

SERVANT
I do, Mark Antony.

MARK ANTONY
Caesar has ordered him to come to Rome.

SERVANT
He has received his letters and is coming,
And said to say to you in person that—[Sees the body]   280
O Caesar!—

MARK ANTONY
Your heart is swollen. Stand aside and weep.
Grief, I'm afraid, is catching, and my eyes,
Seeing those beads of sorrow there on yours,
Began to water. Is your master coming?   285

SERVANT
He's camped tonight some twenty miles from Rome.

MARK ANTONY
Race back and tell him what has happened here.
This is a mourning Rome, a dangerous Rome,
A Rome not safe yet for Octavius.
Hurry, and tell him. Better yet, hold on.   290
Don't leave until I carry his remains
Into the market-place. My eulogy
Will let me test how people there regard
The cruel product of these bloody men,
A finding you'll include in your report   295
To young Octavius on the state of things.
Give me a hand.

[Exit with JULIUS CAESAR's body]

Scene Two. The Forum

[Enter BRUTUS and CASSIUS,
with a crowd of PLEBEIANS]

PLEBEIANS
Explain this. We demand an explanation.

BRUTUS
Then follow me, and listen to me, friends.—
Cassius, you go on down the other street
To split the crowd up.—
Those wishing to hear me, let them stay here;   5
And those who'll follow Cassius, go with him;
And then a public statement will be made
On Caesar's death.

FIRST PLEBEIAN
                I'll hear what Brutus says.

SECOND PLEBEIAN
I'll go hear Cassius and compare the reasons
They give when they are speaking separately.   10

[Exit CASSIUS, with some of the PLEBEIANS]

[BRUTUS steps up on the rostrum]

THIRD PLEBEIAN
The noble Brutus has ascended. Silence!

BRUTUS
Be calm until I finish.
Romans, countrymen, and dear friends, listen while I explain my actions and remain silent so you can hear. Trust me because I am a man of honor, and keep in mind that my 15
honor is why you trust me. Use your knowledge to judge me and awake your powers of reason so that you may be a better judge. If there is anyone in this assembly, any dear friend of Caesar, to him I say that Brutus' love for Caesar was no less than his. If that friend then demands to know 20
why Brutus rose against Caesar, this is my answer: it's not that I loved Caesar less, but that I loved Rome more. Would you rather Caesar were alive and we all die as slaves, or that Caesar were dead and we all live as freemen? Because Caesar loved me, I weep for him; because he was successful, 25
I rejoice; because he was valiant, I honor him; but because he was too ambitious, I slew him. There are tears for his love, joy for his success, honor for his valor, and death for his ambition. Who here is so low that he would wish to be a bondservant? If any, then speak, for him I have offended. 30
Who here is so barbarous that he would not be a Roman? If any, then speak, for him I have offended. Who here is so vile that he will not love his country? If any, then speak, for him I have offended. I wait for your reply.

PLEBEIANS
None, Brutus, none. 35

BRUTUS
Then none have I offended. I have done no more to Caesar than you would do to Brutus. The circumstances of his death are recorded in the Capitol, his glory, for which he was praised is not diminished, and his offenses, for which he suffered death, are not exaggerated. 40

[Enter MARK ANTONY and others, with Caesar's body]

Here comes his body, mourned by Mark Antony, who, though he had no hand in his death, shall receive the benefits of his dying, a place in a free republic, and which of you shall not have that? I depart with this—that, though I slew my dearest friend for the good of Rome, I keep the 45 same dagger for myself, when it pleases my countrymen to desire my death.

PLEBEIANS
Live, Brutus! Live, live!

FIRST PLEBEIAN
Bring him in triumph back home to his house.

SECOND PLEBEIAN
Give him a statue with his ancestors. 50

THIRD PLEBEIAN
Let him be Caesar.

FOURTH PLEBEIAN
                    Let the best of Caesar
Be crowned in Brutus.

FIRST PLEBEIAN
                    We'll bring him to his house
With cheers and roars.

BRUTUS
My countrymen,—

SECOND PLEBEIAN
                    Peace! Silence! Brutus speaks.

FIRST PLEBEIAN
Quiet, please! 55

BRUTUS
Good countrymen, let me depart alone.
To thank me, please stay here with Antony.
Pay your respects to Caesar and respect
This speech on Caesar's glory, which Antony,

With our permission, is allowed to make.   60
And I insist that not a man depart,
Save I alone, till Antony has spoken.

[He descends from the rostrum and exits]

FIRST PLEBEIAN
Please, stay! And let us hear Mark Antony.

THIRD PLEBEIAN
Let him go up onto the rostrum there.
We'll listen.—Noble Antony, go up.   65

MARK ANTONY
I owe you all a debt now, thanks to Brutus.

[MARK ANTONY ascends the rostrum]

FOURTH PLEBEIAN
What did he say of Brutus?

THIRD PLEBEIAN
                              That thanks to Brutus,
He finds himself indebted to us all.

FOURTH PLEBEIAN
He'd better not speak ill of Brutus here.

FIRST PLEBEIAN
This Caesar was a tyrant.

THIRD PLEBEIAN
                              Yes, that's certain.   70
We're blessed that Rome is rid of him.

SECOND PLEBEIAN
Quiet! Let's hear what Antony will say.

MARK ANTONY
Distinguished Romans—

PLEBEIANS

Quiet, please! Let's listen.

MARK ANTONY

Friends, Romans, countrymen, lend me your ears.
I come to bury Caesar, not to praise him.   75
The evil that men do lives after them;
The good is often buried with their bones.
So let it be with Caesar. The noble Brutus
Has said to you that Caesar was ambitious.[4]
If it is so, then it's a grievous crime,   80
And grievously has Caesar paid for it.
Here, by consent of Brutus and the rest,—
For Brutus is an honorable man,
As are they all, all honorable men—
I've come to speak at Caesar's funeral.   85
He was my friend, faithful and just to me,
But Brutus says that Caesar was ambitious,
And Brutus is an honorable man.
He has brought many captives home to Rome,
Whose ransoms filled the public treasury.   90
Is this why he says Caesar was ambitious?
And when the poor have cried, Caesar has wept;
Ambition should be made of sterner stuff.
Yet Brutus says that Caesar was ambitious,
And Brutus is an honorable man.   95
You saw me at the feast of Lupercal
Present to him three times a kingly crown,
And three times he refused. Was this ambition?
Yet Brutus says that Caesar was ambitious,
And surely he's an honorable man.   100
I'm not here to dispute what Brutus said,
But I am here to tell you what I know.
I know you loved him once—not without cause.
What cause prevents you now from mourning him?—
O judgment, you have fled toward brutish beasts,   105
And men have lost their reason! [weeps]—Bear with me.
My heart is in the coffin there with Caesar,
And I must pause till it comes back to me.

FIRST PLEBEIAN
There seems to be some sense in what he's saying.

SECOND PLEBEIAN
If you consider carefully this matter,   110
Caesar's been greatly wronged.

THIRD PLEBEIAN
              He has indeed.
I fear that something worse will take his place.

FOURTH PLEBEIAN
Did you hear that? He would not take the crown.
That means it's certain he was not ambitious.

FIRST PLEBEIAN
If we can prove it, someone must pay dearly.   115

SECOND PLEBEIAN
Poor soul! His eyes are red as fire from weeping.

THIRD PLEBEIAN
There's not a nobler man in Rome than Antony.

FOURTH PLEBEIAN
Now listen. He's about to speak again.

MARK ANTONY
Just yesterday the word of Caesar might
Have stood up to the world. Now he lies there,   120
The lowest now too high to show respect.
O masters, if I were inclined to stir
Your hearts and minds to mutiny and rage,
It might wrong Brutus and wrong Cassius,
Who, you all know, are honorable men.   125
I do not wish to wrong them and would choose
To wrong the dead, to wrong myself, and you,
Before I'd wrong such honorable men.
But here's a document with Caesar's seal—
I found it in his study—it's his will.   130

If citizens could hear his testament—
Forgive me, but I don't intend to read it—
Then they would go and kiss dead Caesar's wounds,
And dip their kerchiefs in his sacred blood,
Yes, sneak a strand of hair for memory,   135
And, dying, mention it within their wills,
Bequeathing it as a rich legacy
Unto their offspring.

FOURTH PLEBEIAN
We want to hear it. Read it, Antony.

CITIZENS
The will, the will! We want to hear the will.   140

MARK ANTONY
Have patience, gentle friends. I must not read it.
It's fitting you don't know how Caesar loved you.
You are not wood, you are not stones, but men.
And, being men, if you hear Caesar's will,
It will inflame you; it will make you mad.   145
It's good you do not know that you're his heirs,
For if you did, O, what would come of it!

FOURTH CITIZEN
Read it! We want to hear it, Antony.
You must read us the will—Caesar's will!

MARK ANTONY
Will you be patient? Will you wait awhile?   150
I've gone too far by mentioning it to you.
I fear I'll wrong the honorable men
Whose daggers have stabbed Caesar. I do fear it.

FOURTH CITIZEN
They were traitors. Honorable men!

CITIZENS
The will! The testament!   155

SECOND CITIZEN
They were villains, murderers. The will! Read the will!

MARK ANTONY
You truly wish to make me read the will?
Then make a ring around the corpse of Caesar,
And let me show you all who made the will.
May I descend? Do I have your consent?   160

CITIZENS
Come down.

SECOND PLEBEIAN
Descend.

THIRD PLEBEIAN
You have permission.

    [MARK ANTONY comes down from the rostrum]

FOURTH PLEBEIAN
A ring. Stand in a ring.

FIRST PLEBEIAN
Back from the coffin. Back from the body.   165

SECOND PLEBEIAN
Make room for Antony, most noble Antony!

MARK ANTONY
No, not so close around me—farther back.

PLEBEIANS
Stand back! Make room! Move back!

MARK ANTONY
If you have tears, prepare to shed them now.
You recognize this robe. I can remember   170
The very first time Caesar put it on.
It was a summer evening, in his tent,
The day he overcame the Nervii tribe.[5]
Look, here's where Cassius' dagger went.
Look at the rip the spiteful Casca made.   175
Through this the well-belovèd Brutus cut,
And as he plucked his cursèd steel blade out,

Note how the blood of Caesar followed it,
As if it rushed outside the door to see
If such an unkind knock had come from Brutus,   180
For Brutus, as you know, was Caesar's angel.
Judge, O you gods, how dearly Caesar loved him!
This was the most unkindest cut of all.
For when the noble Caesar saw him stab,
It was ingratitude, much stronger than   185
These traitors' arms that vanquished him and burst
His mighty heart. His robe thrown up around
His face, there at the base of Pompey's statue,
All running with his blood, great Caesar fell.
O, what a fall that was, my countrymen!   190
There I, and you, and all of us fell down,
With bloody treason brandished over us.
Yes, now you weep, and I can see you feel
A blast of pity. These are fitting drops.
Kind souls, these wounds you see in Caesar's clothes,   195
Do they alone cause you to weep? Look here.

[He lifts up Caesar's robe]

He's here—and mutilated by these traitors.

FIRST PLEBEIAN
A pitiful spectacle!

SECOND PLEBEIAN
O noble Caesar!

THIRD PLEBEIAN
An awful day!   200

FOURTH PLEBEIAN
O traitors, villains!

FIRST PLEBEIAN
O a bloody sight!

SECOND PLEBEIAN
We will have revenge.

PLEBEIANS
Revenge! Let's go! Find them. Burn! Set fires! Kill! Slay
them! No traitor left alive!   205

MARK ANTONY
Wait, countrymen.

FIRST PLEBEIAN
Quiet! Listen to noble Antony.

SECOND PLEBEIAN
We'll listen, we'll follow him, we'll die with him.

MARK ANTONY
Good friends, sweet friends, do not let me stir up
In you a sudden flood of violence.   210
Those who have done this deed are honorable.
What private grudges led to this, alas,
I do not know. They're wise and honorable,
And will, no doubt, explain their reasoning.
I'm not here, friends, to steal away your hearts.   215
I am no orator, as Brutus is,
But am—as you all know—a plain, blunt man
Who loved a friend, a fact known well by those
Who let me come to speak of him in public.
I lack the cleverness, the words, or weight,   220
The gestures, diction, or delivery
To stir men's blood. I only say it straight.
I tell you things that you already know.
I show sweet Caesar's wounds—poor silent mouths—
And have them speak for me. But were I Brutus,   225
And Brutus Antony, this Antony
Would then enrage your spirits and put a tongue
In each of Caesar's wounds, so as to move
The stones of Rome to rise in mutiny.

PLEBEIANS
We'll riot.   230

FIRST PLEBEIAN
We'll burn the house of Brutus.

THIRD PLEBEIAN
Let's go, then! We'll find the conspirators.

MARK ANTONY
Countrymen, listen. I have more to say.

PLEBEIANS
Quiet! And listen to our noble Antony!

MARK ANTONY
Please, friends, you're off to do you know not what.   235
In what ways has great Caesar earned your love?
Alas, you do not know, so I must tell you.
Did you forget the will I told you of?

PLEBEIANS
That's right. The will!—Let's wait and hear the will.

MARK ANTONY
Here is the will, and under Caesar's seal.   240
To every Roman citizen he gives,
To every single man, seventy-five drachmas.

SECOND PLEBEIAN
Most noble Caesar!—We'll revenge his death.

THIRD PLEBEIAN
O, royal Caesar!

MARK ANTONY
Now listen calmly.   245

PLEBEIANS
Quiet, now!

MARK ANTONY
He also leaves you all his promenades,
His summer rests, and freshly-planted gardens
Along the Tiber. These he leaves to you
And to your heirs forever—public parks   250
To walk around in and refresh yourselves.
This was a Caesar! When will there be another?

FIRST PLEBEIAN
Never, never! Come on. Let's go. Let's go!
We'll burn his body in a holy place,
And with the coals ignite the traitors' houses.   255
Lift up the body.

SECOND PLEBEIAN
Go, fetch some fire.

THIRD PLEBEIAN
Pull down benches.

FOURTH PLEBEIAN
Pull down bleachers, shutters, anything.

          [Exit PLEBEIANS, with the body]

MARK ANTONY
Now do your work.—Mischief, you're now released   260
And free to choose your path!

          [Enter a SERVANT]

                    What is it, fellow?

SERVANT
Sir, Octavius is here in Rome already.

MARK ANTONY
Where is he?

SERVANT
He and Lepidus are at Caesar's house.

MARK ANTONY
Then I'll go there at once to visit him.   265
Just as I wished. The goddess Fortune's merry,
And in this mood, she'll give us anything.

SERVANT
I heard him say Brutus and Cassius
Rode off like madmen through the gates of Rome.

MARK ANTONY
It's likely they got word of how I have   270
Aroused the people. Take me to Octavius.

[Exit]

Scene Three. Rome. A Street

[Enter a POET]

POET (also named Cinna)
I dreamt last night I had a feast with Caesar,
And ominous things haunt my imagination.
I do not want to wander out of doors,
Yet something draws me out.

[Enter PLEBEIANS]

FIRST PLEBEIAN
What is your name?   5

SECOND PLEBEIAN
Where are you going?

THIRD PLEBEIAN
Where do you live?

FOURTH PLEBEIAN
Are you a married man or a bachelor?

SECOND PLEBEIAN
Answer every man directly.

FIRST PLEBEIAN
Yes, and briefly. 10

FOURTH PLEBEIAN
Yes, and wisely.

THIRD PLEBEIAN
Yes, and it better be the truth.

POET
What is my name? Where am I going? Where do I live? Am I a married man or a bachelor? And I'm to answer every man directly and briefly, wisely and truthfully. I'll start 15 wisely and say that I am a bachelor.

SECOND PLEBEIAN
That's the same as saying that those who marry are fools. You'll get a blow from me for that, I'm afraid. Continue but more directly.

POET
I'm going directly to Caesar's funeral. 20

FIRST PLEBEIAN
As a friend, or an enemy?

POET
As a friend.

SECOND PLEBEIAN
That question was answered directly.

FOURTH PLEBEIAN
And where you live—briefly.

POET
I've lived briefly near the Capitol.   25

THIRD PLEBEIAN
Your name, sir,—the truth.

POET
My true name is Cinna.

FIRST PLEBEIAN
Tear him to pieces! He's a conspirator.

POET
I am Cinna the poet, I am Cinna the poet.

FOURTH PLEBEIAN
Then tear him apart for writing bad verses, tear him apart   30
for his bad verses.

POET
I am not Cinna the conspirator.

FOURTH PLEBEIAN
It makes no difference. His name's Cinna. So pry only his
name out of his heart, and send him off.

THIRD PLEBEIAN
Tear him to pieces, tear him apart! Come and bring the   35
torches! To Brutus', to Cassius'. Burn them all. Some of you
go to Decius' house, and some to Casca's, some to Ligarius'!
Let's go!

[Exit the PLEBEIANS, dragging the POET along]

Julius Caesar

Act Four

Act Four

[MARK ANTONY, OCTAVIUS, and LEPIDUS,
seated at a table]

MARK ANTONY (member of the Triumvirate)
This many then shall die. I've marked their names.

OCTAVIUS (member of the Triumvirate)
Your brother's name's here, Lepidus. Agreed?

LEPIDUS (member of the Triumvirate)
Yes, I agree—

OCTAVIUS
        Mark him down, Antony.

LEPIDUS
—On this condition: that your sister's son,
Publius, shall not live, Mark Antony.   5

MARK ANTONY
He shall not live. [places a mark on the list] See, with a
   tick I damn him.
And, Lepidus, go down to Caesar's house.
Bring back the will, and we'll look for a way
To fund some of these costs out of the proceeds.

LEPIDUS
Will I still find you here?   10

OCTAVIUS
You'll find us here or at the Capitol.

[Exit LEPIDUS]

MARK ANTONY
He is a weak and undeserving man,
Fit to be sent on errands. Is it right
To split the world in thirds and let him stand
As one of three who shares it?

OCTAVIUS
               You hold this view,   15
Yet during our harsh sentencing you let
Him pick who should be killed and who'd be exiled.

MARK ANTONY
Octavius, I've seen more days than you,
And though we've laid these honors on this man
To ease the burden of all sorts of blame,   20
He hauls them like a donkey hauling gold,
To groan and sweat while toiling under it.
He's led or driven, while we point the way,
And once he's brought our treasure where we want,
We then lift down his load and set him loose,   25
A donkey with no pack, to shake his ears
And graze out on the commons.

OCTAVIUS
               As you wish,
But he's a tested and a valiant soldier.

MARK ANTONY
So is my horse, Octavius, and for that
I keep him properly supplied with feed.   30
It is a creature that I teach to fight,
To turn, to stop, to run in a straight line,
His bodily motion governed by my mind.
And that is Lepidus to some extent.
He must be taught and trained and prodded on—   35
A fellow with a barren mind, who feeds
On trinkets, curios, and imitations,
Discarded and worn out by other men,
Which he thinks are the fashion. See him as
A tool we use. And now, Octavius,   40

Important things. Brutus and Cassius
Are raising armies. We must move right now,
So let's unite into an allied force
With our best friends' support, stretch our supplies,
And meet at once in private to decide   45
How unknown risks can best be ascertained
And obvious perils safely circumvented.

OCTAVIUS
Let's do this. We are tied up to a stake
With baying enemies on every side,
And some who smile have in their hearts, I fear,   50
A million kinds of malice.

[Exit]

Scene Two. Near Sardis. In Front of Brutus' Tent

[Drums sound. Enter BRUTUS, LUCILIUS, TITINIUS,
and SOLDIERS; PINDARUS meeting them;
LUCIUS at some distance]

BRUTUS
Halt!

LUCILIUS (an officer)
Pass the word along, and halt.

BRUTUS
Lucilius, any word? Is Cassius near?

LUCILIUS
He is nearby, and Pindarus has come
To bring a formal greeting from his master.   5

[PINDARUS gives a letter to Brutus]

BRUTUS
A good man brings it.—Your master, Pindarus,
Due to changed feelings or bad officers,

Has given me just cause to wish some things
Be done and not done, but if he is nearby,
I need an explanation.

PINDARUS (servant to Cassius)
      I am sure   10
My noble master will, just as before,
Be quite deserving of respect and honor.[1]

BRUTUS
I'm sure he will.

    [turns to speak with LUCILIUS]

     Your thoughts, Lucilius
On how you were received. Clear up these doubts.

LUCILIUS
He paid attention and was courteous   15
But with less intimacy than before,
And with less frank and friendly conversation
Than normal in the past.

BRUTUS
     You have described
A warm friend cooling. Typically, Lucilius,
When love begins to sicken and decay,   20
It shows a strained formality—in plain
And simple oaths there are no fancy words.
But hollow men, like horses hot to charge,
Put on a gallant show of promised spirit,
Yet when they must endure the bloody spur,   25
They drop their necks, and, like deceitful nags
Fail in the trial. Is his army here?

LUCILIUS
Tonight they plan to set up camp in Sardis.
The bulk of it, most of the cavalry,
Have come with Cassius.

    [The sound of marching is heard]

BRUTUS
      Listen! He's arrived.   30
March calmly out to meet him.

   [Enter CASSIUS and SOLDIERS]

CASSIUS
Halt!

BRUTUS
Halt! Pass the word along.

FIRST SOLDIER
Halt!

SECOND SOLDIER
Halt!   35

THIRD SOLDIER
Halt!

CASSIUS
Most noble brother, you have done me wrong.

BRUTUS
Gods, judge me. I have yet to hurt a foe,
So how is it that I have wronged a brother?

CASSIUS
Brutus, this dignity of yours hides wrongs, 40
And when you do them—

BRUTUS
      Cassius, be calm.
State your complaints more softly. We are friends.
We're where the eyes of both our armies see us,
Where nothing but our love should be observed,
So let's not wrangle. Have them move away. 45
Then in my tent, Cassius, you're free to talk
And I'll pay close attention.

CASSIUS
                    Pindarus,
Have our commanders tell their troops to move
Some distance from this spot.

BRUTUS
Lucilius, do the same, and let no man   50
Approach our tent till our discussion's over.
Lucius and Titinius, guard our door.

[Exit all]

Scene Three. Inside Brutus' Tent

[Enter BRUTUS and CASSIUS]

CASSIUS
The fact you've wronged me's rather evident
When you convict and tarnish Lucius Pella
For taking bribes here from the Sardians
But disregard my letters where I plead
On his behalf because I knew the man.   5

BRUTUS
You wronged yourself by taking up his case.

CASSIUS
This hardly seems the proper time to come
Down hard on every trivial infraction.

BRUTUS
Now listen, Cassius. I hear complaints
That you yourself have quite the itchy palm,   10
And fill appointments with the undeserving,
Who pay for them with gold.

CASSIUS
                    An itchy palm?
You know if it weren't Brutus saying this,
Then, by the gods, these words would be your last.

BRUTUS
Your name brings so much honor to this racket
That punishment has gone and hid its head.   15

CASSIUS
Punishment?

BRUTUS
Remember March, the ides of March. Remember.
We made great Julius bleed for justice, right?
Was there a villain there who touched—who stabbed—
His body not for justice? Which of us   20
Who struck the foremost man in all the world,
A man who coddled thieves, would have us now
Contaminate our fingers with base bribes
And sell the vast expanse of our great status
For just whatever trash our hands can grab?   25
Better chained up and baying at the moon,
Than be that kind of Roman.

CASSIUS
                              Don't chain me.
I won't allow it. It is not your place
To hedge me in like this. I am a soldier,
With more seniority and more adept   30
In practical affairs.

BRUTUS
                    That's nonsense, Cassius.

CASSIUS
I am.

BRUTUS
I say you are not.

CASSIUS
Provoke me and I may forget myself.
Think of your welfare. Do not tempt me further.   35

BRUTUS
Leave, you trifler!

CASSIUS
Can this be real?

BRUTUS
        You're going to listen now.
Must I step back and yield to your rash anger?
Should I be frightened when a madman glares?

CASSIUS
O gods, you gods, must I endure all this?   40

BRUTUS
All this? And more. Rage till your proud heart breaks.
Go show your slaves how full of fire you are.
Make all who serve you tremble. Should I flinch?
Must I show deference? Should I stand and cower
Beneath your nasty temper? By the gods,   45
You can choke down the venom from your spleen
Until you burst because from this day forth,
I'll use you for amusement. Yes, I'll laugh
When you're this touchy.

CASSIUS
              Has it come to this?

BRUTUS
You say you are a better soldier, right?   50
Then let me see it. Show it's not a boast,
And I will be delighted. As for me,
I'll be quite glad to learn from noble men.

CASSIUS
You wrong me, Brutus, and in every way.
I said a senior soldier, not a better.   55
Did I say "better"?

BRUTUS
        If so, I don't care.

CASSIUS
When Caesar lived, he did not dare to rile me.

BRUTUS
You wouldn't dare provoke him in this way.

CASSIUS
I wouldn't?

BRUTUS
No.   60

CASSIUS
Dare to provoke him?

BRUTUS
                              No, not on your life.

CASSIUS
Don't count too much upon my love for you.
I may do something I'll be sorry for.

BRUTUS
You have done something to be sorry for.
There is no terror, Cassius, in your threats.   65
The armor of my virtue is so strong
Threats pass me by just like an idle breeze
To which I pay no heed. I sent to you
For certain sums of gold—which you denied me—
Since I can't raise it in dishonest ways.   70
By god, I'd rather turn my heart to coins
And spill my blood for drachmas than to wring
Some measly cash from peasant's hard-worn hands
By any devious means—And so I sent
For gold to pay my legions, gold which you   75
Denied me. How is that like Cassius?
Would I have treated Caius Cassius so?
When Marcus Brutus grows so greedy as
To lock away such meager change from friends,
Be ready, gods, with all your thunderbolts—   80
Dash him to pieces!

CASSIUS
                              I did not deny you.

BRUTUS
You did.

CASSIUS
No, I did not. Some fool confused the message
That I sent back. Brutus has crushed my heart.
A friend accepts shortcomings in a friend,   85
But Brutus makes mine greater than they are.

BRUTUS
I don't until you try them out on me.

CASSIUS
You do not love me.

BRUTUS
                I don't like your faults.

CASSIUS
A friendly eye would never see these faults.

BRUTUS
A flatterer would not, though they appear   90
As huge as Mt. Olympus.

CASSIUS
Come, Antony and young Octavius, come.
Get your revenge on Cassius alone,
For Cassius has grown weary of the world—
Defied and hated by a loving brother;   95
Rebuked like some mere slave; his faults observed,
Recorded in a notebook, learned by rote,
And forced back down my throat. O, I could cry
All life out of my eyes! Here is my dagger,
And here's my naked breast, a heart inside   100
More precious than the gold in Pluto's mines.
If you're a man of Rome, then take it out.
I, who denied you gold, will give my heart.
Strike me as you did Caesar. For I know
That when you hated Caesar most, your love   105
Was greater than it is for me.

BRUTUS
              Sheathe your dagger.
Be angry when you want. It must run free.
It's what you do. These insults are your way.
O Cassius, you're yoked up to a lamb
Who stores his anger much like flint holds fire.   110
When sharply struck, it quickly shows a spark,
But soon is cold again.

CASSIUS
              Is Cassius here
Just so his grief and his ill-tempered blood
When stirred will give some laughter to his Brutus?

BRUTUS
When I said that, I was ill-tempered too.   115

CASSIUS
Will you admit this much? Give me your hand.

BRUTUS
And my heart too.

CASSIUS
            O Brutus,—

BRUTUS
                What's the matter?

CASSIUS
Do you have love enough to bear with me
When this rash nature which my mother gave me
Makes me forget myself?

BRUTUS
            Yes, from now on,   120
When you are too severe with me, I'll hear
Your mother scolding me and let it go.

           [Noise outside the tent]

POET
[Outside the tent] Let me go in to see the generals.
There's some dispute between them. It is best
They're not alone.

LUCILIUS
             [Outside] You're not allowed to enter.   125

POET
[Outside] Nothing but death shall stop me.

[Enter a POET, followed by LUCILIUS, and TITINIUS]

CASSIUS
What's this? What's the matter?

POET
Come now, you generals! What is all this?
Love and be friends, as two such men should do,
For I have seen more years, I'm sure, than you.   130

CASSIUS
Ha, ha! How terribly this critic rhymes!

BRUTUS
Get out you clown. You insolent fellow, out!

CASSIUS
Now calm down, Brutus. It is just his way.

BRUTUS
Now's not the time for eccentricities.
What good are these fools' jingles in a war?—   135
Get out, you lout!

CASSIUS
             Away, away, be gone!

[Exit POET]

BRUTUS
Lucilius and Titinius, tell the commanders
To have their units make camp for tonight.

CASSIUS
Then come back here immediately and bring
Messala with you.   140

[Exit LUCILIUS and TITINIUS]

BRUTUS
[To LUCIUS outside] Lucius, a bowl of wine!

CASSIUS
It doesn't seem that you should be so angry.

BRUTUS
O Cassius, these problems wear me down.

CASSIUS
You're not the stoic that you used to be
If you're this overwhelmed by chance misfortune.   145

BRUTUS
No man bears sorrow better. Portia is dead.

CASSIUS
What? Portia?

BRUTUS
She is dead.

CASSIUS
How could you spare me when I riled you so?—
What an unbearable and piercing loss!—   150
What sickness was it?

BRUTUS
                    The burden of my absence
And grief that young Octavius and Mark Antony
Have made themselves so strong—the same dispatch
Had news of this—these drove her to distraction.
With her attendants out, she swallowed coals.   155

CASSIUS
That's how she died?

BRUTUS
That's how.

CASSIUS
O, you immortal gods!

[Enter LUCIUS, with wine and a candle]

BRUTUS
Speak no more of her.—Give me a bowl of wine.—
In this I bury all bad feelings, Cassius.   160

[Drinks]

CASSIUS
My heart has thirsted for this noble toast.
Pour, Lucius, till wine spills from the cup;
I cannot drink too much of Brutus' love.

[Drinks]
[Exit LUCIUS]
[Enter TITINIUS, with MESSALA]

BRUTUS
Come in, Titinius!—Welcome, good Messala.—
We'll huddle now around this candle here   165
And privately discuss what we must do.

CASSIUS
Portia, are you gone?

BRUTUS
                    No more, I beg you.—
Messala, I have letters here that say
That young Octavius and Mark Antony
Are heading toward us with a mighty force,   170
Advancing toward Philippi rapidly.

MESSALA (an officer)
I too have letters that report the same.

BRUTUS
With anything to add?

MESSALA
By listing them as outlaws with no rights
Octavius, Antony, and Lepidus   175
Have put to death a hundred senators.

BRUTUS
On that our letters do not quite agree.
Mine speaks of seventy consigned to die
With Cicero among these senators.

CASSIUS
Cicero's one?

MESSALA
                        Cicero is dead,   180
And listed by that order as an outlaw.—
Did you get letters from your wife, my lord?[2]

BRUTUS
No, Messala.

MESSALA
And nothing in your letters spoke of her?

BRUTUS
Nothing, Messala.

MESSALA
                        That, to me, seems strange.   185

BRUTUS
Why ask this? Did your letters speak of her?

MESSALA
No, my lord.

BRUTUS
Now, as a Roman, tell me what you know.

MESSALA
Then, like a Roman, bear what I must tell you.
It's certain she has died, in a strange way.   190

BRUTUS
Then farewell, Portia. We must die, Messala.
By thinking she will have to die someday,
I have the self-control to stand it now.

MESSALA
It's how great men can stand a loss so great.

CASSIUS
Although I share the same philosophy,   195
My nature could not handle it like you.

BRUTUS
Well, back to what's alive. What do you think
Of marching to Phillipi at first light?

CASSIUS
I do not think it's good.

BRUTUS
Your reason?   200

CASSIUS
It's this: it's better if the enemy seeks us.
Then he will waste supplies, wear out his soldiers,
And harm himself, while we just stay in place,
Well-rested, well defended, and alert.

BRUTUS
Good reasons by necessity must yield   205
To better ones. Between here and Philippi
The people show allegiance if they're forced,
But they will only grudgingly supply us.
The enemy, while marching through their land,
Will see his numbers grow as he advances,   210
Refreshed, with new troops added, and encouraged.
But that advantage is denied to him

If we can face him at Philippi with
These people at our back.

CASSIUS
              Good brother, listen.

BRUTUS
Allow me to go on. And don't forget   215
That we have asked the utmost of our friends,
Our ranks are brimming, and the moment's right.
The enemy's increasing every day;
We're at our peak and ready to decline.
There is a tide in the affairs of men.   220
When taken at its height, it leads to fortune;
When missed, the voyage of their entire life
Is stranded in the shallows and misfortune.
It's on so full a sea that we now float,
And we must ride the current when it's there   225
Or lose what's ventured.

CASSIUS
             Then go on, as you wish.
We'll come along and face them at Philippi.

BRUTUS
The deep of night has crept upon our talk,
And human nature must obey its needs,
To which we'll now dole out a little rest.   230
Is there still more to say?

CASSIUS
             No more. Good night.
Early tomorrow will we rise and march.

BRUTUS
Lucius!

             [Enter LUCIUS]

My robe.
             [Exit LUCIUS]

Farewell now, good Messala.
Good night, Titinius. Noble, noble Cassius,
Good night. You all sleep well.

CASSIUS
O my dear brother! 235
There was a poor beginning to this night.
Never should such a rift divide our souls!
Don't let it, Brutus.

BRUTUS
Everything is fine.

CASSIUS
Good night, my lord.

BRUTUS
Good night, good brother. 240

TITINIUS (an officer) and MESSALA
Good night, Lord Brutus.

BRUTUS
Farewell, everyone.

[Exit CASSIUS, TITINIUS, and MESSALA]
[Re-enter LUCIUS, with the robe]

Give me the robe. Where is your instrument?

LUCIUS
Here in the tent.

BRUTUS
Oh my, you sound so drowsy.
Poor lad, you're not to blame. You're up too late.
Call Claudius and get some other men. 245
I'll have them sleep on cushions in my tent.

LUCIUS
Varro and Claudius!

[Enter VARRO and CLAUDIUS]

VARRO (a soldier)
Did my lord call?

BRUTUS
Sirs, if you would, please sleep here in my tent
In case I need to wake and send you out   250
On business with my brother Cassius.

VARRO (a soldier)
We'll stand here, as you wish, until you call.

BRUTUS
No, that's not what I wish. Lie down, good sirs.
It's possible that I will change my mind.
Look, Lucius, here's the book I couldn't find.   255
I'd put it in the pocket of my robe.

[LUCIUS and VARRO lie down]

LUCIUS
I was sure your lordship never gave it to me.

BRUTUS
Bear with me, good boy. I'm quite forgetful.
Can you hold up your heavy lids awhile
And pick a tune or two upon your lute?   260

LUCIUS
Ay, my lord, if it pleases you.

BRUTUS
                           It does.
I trouble you too much, but you are willing.

LUCIUS
It is my duty, sir.

BRUTUS
I shouldn't push your duty past your strength.
I know young blood requires a time for rest.   265

LUCIUS
I slept, my lord, already.

BRUTUS
It's good you did, and you shall sleep some more.
I will not keep you long. If I live on,
I will be good to you.

[LUCIUS plays and sings until he falls asleep]

This is a sleepy tune.—O murderous Slumber,   270
You drop your lead-filled club upon a boy
Who plays you music?—Gentle lad, good night.
I'd do you too much wrong were I to wake you.
But if you slump, you'll break your instrument.
I'll take it from you and, good boy, good night.   275
Let's see. Let's see. I think I marked the spot
Where I stopped reading. Here it is, I think.

[Enter CAESAR'S GHOST]

How low this candle's burning! Ha! Who's there?
It has to be the weakness of my eyes
That's formed this monstrous apparition here.   280
It's coming toward me.—Are you something real?
Are you some god, some angel, or some devil
Who's making my blood cold and hair stand up?
Speak. Tell me what you are.

CAESAR'S GHOST
Your evil spirit, Brutus.

BRUTUS
                              Why come here?   285

CAESAR'S GHOST
To tell you that you'll see me at Philippi.

BRUTUS
Then I'll be seeing you again?

CAESAR'S GHOST
Yes, at Philippi.

BRUTUS
Well, I will see you at Philippi then.

[CAESAR'S GHOST vanishes]

My nerve returns and then you disappear.   290
You evil ghost, I'd like more words with you.
Boy! Lucius!—Varro! Claudius! Sirs, awake!—Claudius!

LUCIUS
The strings, my lord, are out of tune.

BRUTUS
He thinks that he's still with his instrument.
Lucius, wake up!   295

LUCIUS
My lord?

BRUTUS
Did your dreams, Lucius, cause you to cry out?

The Plains of Philippi

LUCIUS
My lord, I didn't know that I cried out.

BRUTUS
Indeed, you did. Did you see anything?

LUCIUS
Nothing, my lord.   300

BRUTUS
Go back to sleep.—You there, Claudius!—
[To VARRO] Fellow, wake up!

VARRO
My lord?

CLAUDIUS
My lord?

BRUTUS
What made you cry like that, sirs, in your sleep?   305

VARRO and CLAUDIUS
Did we, my lord?

BRUTUS
You did. Did you see anything?

VARRO
No, my lord, I saw nothing.

CLAUDIUS
Nor I, my lord.

BRUTUS
Go send my greetings to my brother Cassius.   310
Order him to advance ahead of us,
And we will follow.

VARRO and CLAUDIUS
It shall be done, my lord.

                    [Exit all]

Julius Caesar

Act Five

Act Five

Scene One. The Plains of Philippi

[Enter OCTAVIUS, MARK ANTONY, and their army]

OCTAVIUS
Now, Antony, they've answered all our moves.
You said the enemy would not come down
But hold instead the hills and higher ground.
That's not the case. Their battle lines are formed
Here at Philippi where they'll challenge us   5
And spoil our assault before it's made.

MARK ANTONY
Relax. I'm deep inside their heads and know
Why they are doing this. I know they'd like
To launch from several places and attack
With fierce bravado, thinking such a sight   10
Will force our minds to think that they have courage.
It's not to be.

[Enter a MESSENGER]

MESSENGER
                    Be ready, generals.
The enemy's nearby in grand display,
They've hung their bloody flag of battle out,
And something must be done immediately.   15

MARK ANTONY
Octavius, move your forces slowly up,
Along the left side where the field is level.

125

OCTAVIUS
I'll go along the right; you take the left.

MARK ANTONY
Why contradict me at this crucial time?

OCTAVIUS
I'm not, but still I want to take the right.   20

[Drums. Enter BRUTUS, CASSIUS, and their army; LU-
    CILIUS, TITINIUS, MESSALA, and OTHERS]

BRUTUS
They're holding and wish to negotiate.

CASSIUS
Stay put, Titinius. We'll come out and talk.

OCTAVIUS
Mark Antony, shall we show flags of battle?

MARK ANTONY
No, Caesar, we'll respond when they attack.
Step forward, so these generals can speak.   25

OCTAVIUS
Hold steady till the signal.

BRUTUS
Words before blows. Is that right, countrymen?

OCTAVIUS
Not that we love words better, as you do.

BRUTUS
Good words are better than bad blows, Octavius.

MARK ANTONY
With your bad blows, Brutus, we hear fine words.   30
Recall the hole you made in Caesar's heart,
While crying, "Long live, Caesar!"

CASSIUS

                       Antony,
The nature of your blows is still unknown;
As for your words, they rob the finest bees,
And leave them honeyless.

MARK ANTONY

                 And stingless too?   35

BRUTUS
O, yes, and soundless,
You even steal their buzzing, Antony,
And wisely send alerts before you sting.

MARK ANTONY
Villains! You sent him none when your vile daggers
Hacked one-by-one into the sides of Caesar.   40
You showed your teeth like apes, and fawned like
    hounds,
And bowed like servants, kissing Caesar's feet,
While from behind, damned Casca, like a dog,
Struck Caesar on the neck. O flatterers!

CASSIUS
Flatterers!—Brutus, thank yourself for this.   45
This tongue could not offend us so today
If Cassius had prevailed.

OCTAVIUS
Come to the point. If arguing makes us sweat,
The test is when the drops start turning red.
Look,— [he draws his sword]   50
I draw my sword against conspirators;
When do you think I'll sheathe this sword again?
Never, till Caesar's three and thirty wounds
Are well avenged, or till this Caesar too
Is added to the slaughter done by traitors.   55

BRUTUS
Caesar, you cannot die by traitors' hands,
Unless you've brought them with you.

OCTAVIUS
                                          As I hoped.
I was not born to die from Brutus' sword.

BRUTUS
O, if you were the noblest in your line,
Young man, you could not die more honorably.   60

CASSIUS
A foolish school boy, far beneath such honor,
Joined by a party-goer in a mask!

MARK ANTONY
The same old Cassius!

OCTAVIUS
                              Let's go, Antony!
Traitors, we hurl defiance in your teeth.
If you dare fight today, come to the field.   65
If not, then when your stomach's ready.

    [Exit OCTAVIUS, MARK ANTONY, and their ARMY]

CASSIUS
The wind now blows, waves swell, and boats will sail!
The storm is up, and everything's at risk.

BRUTUS
Ho, Lucilius! Here, a word with you.

LUCILIUS
My lord?   70

        [BRUTUS and LUCILIUS talk apart]

CASSIUS
Messala,—

MESSALA
              Yes, my General?

CASSIUS
                                        Messala,
This is my birthday. On this very day
Was Cassius born. Give me your hand, Messala.
You are my witness that against my will,
As Pompey was, I am compelled to risk   75
In just one battle all our liberties.
You know I share the views of Epicurus,[1]
But now I've changed my mind and partly think
That gods send omens of what is to come.
As we left Sardis, on our foremost banner   80
Two mighty eagles landed. There they perched,
Gorging and feeding from our soldiers' hands,
And travelled to Philippi with our troops.
This morning they have flown away and gone,
And in their place now ravens, crows, and kites   85
Fly overhead while looking down on us
As if we're soon their prey. Their shadows seem
A shroud most ominous, and under it
Our army lies, ready to give up the ghost.

MESSALA
You can't believe this.

CASSIUS
                                    Only part of it.   90
My spirit's full of hope, and I'm resolved
To meet all perils without wavering.

BRUTUS
[while rejoining CASSIUS] Indeed, Lucilius.

CASSIUS
                                    Now, most noble Brutus,
Let's hope the gods are on our side so we,
Dear friends in peace, can live into old age.   95
But since affairs of men remain uncertain,
Let's contemplate the worst that may befall us.
If we should lose this battle, this will be
The very last time that we'll speak together.

If so, what have you then resolved to do?   100

BRUTUS
The rules of my philosophy demand
That I fault Cato for the life he took
By his own hand—I don't know how but I
Find it both cowardly and vile to fear
What might occur and thus cut short the rest   105
Of life—and so I arm myself with patience
To wait below for what some higher power
Who governs us provides.

CASSIUS
                              Then, if we lose this battle,
You're ready to be led in triumph through
The streets of Rome.   110

BRUTUS
No, Cassius, no. Don't ever think, good Roman,
That Brutus will go bound in chains to Rome.
His mind's too noble. But today it's time
To end the work the ides of March began.
And whether we shall meet again, who knows,   115
So now our everlasting farewell comes.
Forever and forever farewell, Cassius!
If we do meet again, why then we'll smile;
If not, why then our parting was done well.

CASSIUS
Forever and forever farewell, Brutus!   120
If we do meet again, we'll smile indeed;
If not, it's true this parting was done well.

BRUTUS
Why then, lead on. If only one could know
The ending of this day before it comes!
But it suffices that the day will end,   125
And then the end is known. Come ho, away!

[Exit]

Scene Two. The Plains of Philippi. A Battlefield

[A call to arms with trumpets and drums.
Enter BRUTUS and MESSALA]

BRUTUS
Ride, ride, Messala, ride, and get these orders
To the commander on the other flank.

[Loud trumpets and drums]

Let them attack at once, for I can sense
A cooling fervor in Octavius' wing.
A sudden push and we can rout them now.   5
Ride, ride, Messala. Let them all charge down.

[Exit]

Scene Three. Another Part of the Battlefield

[Trumpets and drums sound]
[Enter CASSIUS and TITINIUS]

CASSIUS
O, look, Titinius, look, the rogues are fleeing!
To my own men I'm now an enemy.
The carrier of my banner turned and ran.
I slew the coward; then I took it from him.

TITINIUS
O Cassius, Brutus gave the word too early.   5
He had Octavius at a disadvantage,
But moved too soon. His soldiers started looting
While Antony completely circled us.

[Enter PINDARUS]

PINDARUS
Move farther back, my lord, move farther back.
Mark Antony is in your tents, my lord.   10
Flee, noble Cassius, flee far away.

CASSIUS
This hill is far enough.—Look, look, Titinius,
Are those my tents where I am seeing fire?

TITINIUS
They are, my lord.

CASSIUS
                    Titinius, if you love me,
Then mount my horse and sink your spurs in him   15
Until he's carried you up to those troops,
And then come back so I will know for sure
If those troops there are friend or enemy.

TITINIUS
I'll be back here as quickly as a thought.

                    [Exit TITINIUS]

CASSIUS
Go, Pindarus, get higher on that hill.   20
I've always had poor eyesight. Watch Titinius,
And tell me what you see out on the field.

                    [PINDARUS goes up]

On this day I first breathed. Time has come round,
And where I once began, there I will end;
My life has run its circle.

                    [to PINDARUS above]

                    What can you see?   25

PINDARUS
O my lord!

CASSIUS
What news?

PINDARUS
[Above] A circle has enclosed around Titinius,
With horsemen riding toward him at full spur.
He's spurring hard. They're almost on him now.   30
Titinius! Now some are dismounting. He's dismounting too.
They've got him. [Shouting is heard] Hear that? They're
shouting for joy.

CASSIUS
Come down. Don't watch it any longer.—
A coward's what I am, to live so long,   35
To see my best friend seized before my eyes!

                    [PINDARUS descends]

Come to me, fellow.
In Parthia I took you prisoner
And made you swear for sparing you your life
That anything that I asked you to do   40
You would attempt. It's time to keep that oath.
I set you free, so with this sword that ripped
Through Caesar's entrails, probe into this bosom.
Don't wait to answer. Here, now take the hilt,
And when my face is covered—now it is—   45
Then guide the sword.

                    [PINDARUS stabs him]

                        Caesar, you're now avenged
And by the very sword that killed you.

                    [CASSIUS dies]

PINDARUS
So, I am free, yet it would not be this,
If I had dared do what I want.—O Cassius!

Far from this country Pindarus shall run,   50
Where Romans nevermore will notice him.

[Exit]
[Enter TITINIUS with MESSALA]

MESSALA
A mere exchange, Titinius. For Octavius
Was overthrown by noble Brutus' forces,
As Cassius' legions were by Antony.

TITINIUS
This news would no doubt lift up Cassius.   55

MESSALA
Where did you leave him?

TITINIUS
                              In complete despair,
With Pindarus, his slave, upon this hill.

MESSALA
Is that him lying there upon the ground?

TITINIUS
But not like one who's living. O my heart!

MESSALA
And is it him?

TITINIUS
                   No, this was him, Messala,   60
But Cassius is no more.—O setting sun,
Just as your red rays sink into the night,
So with his red blood, Cassius' day has set,
The sun of Rome has set! Our day is gone.
Clouds, dew, and dangers come. Our deeds are done!   65
Mistrust of my success has done this deed.

MESSALA
Yes, doubts about the outcome did this deed.

O hateful error, melancholy's child!
Why show to men too ready in their thoughts
Things that are not? O error, conceived too soon,   70
You never join us with a happy birth
But kill the mother who delivered you!

TITINIUS
And Pindarus! Where are you, Pindarus?

MESSALA
Find him, Titinius, while I go to meet
The noble Brutus, thrusting this report   75
Into his ears. I can say, "thrusting" it,
For piercing steel and venom-covered darts
Will be as welcome to the ears of Brutus
As tidings of this scene.

TITINIUS
                            Be quick, Messala,
And meanwhile I will search for Pindarus.   80

                [Exit MESSALA]

Why did you send me off, brave Cassius?
Weren't those your friends I met? And didn't they
Place on my brow this wreath of victory
To give to you? You didn't hear their shouts?
A shame—to misinterpret everything!   85
But wait, please wear this garland on your brow.

                [crowns CASSIUS with the wreath]

Your Brutus said that it's for you, and I
Will do his bidding. Brutus, come at once,
And see my high regard for Caius Cassius.—
Permit me, gods to do what Romans must.   90
The sword of Cassius, in my heart I thrust.

                [Stabs himself and dies]

[Trumpets sound]
[Enter BRUTUS, MESSALA, young CATO, STRATO,
VOLUMNIUS, LUCILIUS, LABEO, and FLAVIUS]

BRUTUS
Where, where, Messala, is his body lying?

MESSALA
It's there. Titinius is mourning it.

BRUTUS
Titinius is facing up.

CATO (an officer)
          He's slain.

BRUTUS
O Julius Caesar, mighty you remain.   95
Your spirit roams at large and turns our swords
In our own entrails.

      [Softer trumpets sound, signaling defeat]

CATO
          Brave Titinius!
See if he hasn't crowned dead Cassius!

BRUTUS
Are any Romans left who could match these?—
The last of all the Romans, fare thee well!   100
It's possible that Rome will never breed
An equal to you.—Friends, I owe more tears
To this dead man than you shall see me pay.
I will find time, Cassius, I will find time.
So send his body on to Thasos island.   105
His funeral should not be in our camp,
Lest it discourage us.—Lucilius, come,
And come, young Cato—to the battlefield.
Labeo and Flavius, form our battle lines.

It's three o'clock, and Romans, by tonight   110
We will have tried our luck in a new fight.

[Exit all]

Scene Four. Another Part of the Battlefield

[Trumpets sound. Enter BRUTUS, MESSALA, young
    CATO, LUCILIUS, LABEO, and FLAVIUS]

BRUTUS
On, countrymen, we must not lose our nerve!

[Exit BRUTUS, MESSALA, LABEO, and FLAVIUS]

CATO
Who is so low he would? Who'll go with me?
I will call out my name around the field.
I am the son of Marcus Cato, ho!
A foe to tyrants, and my country's friend.   5
I am the son of Marcus Cato, ho!

[SOLDIERS enter and fight]

LUCILIUS
[to trick the enemy] And I am Brutus, Marcus Brutus, I.
Brutus, my country's friend. Know that I'm Brutus!

[CATO is slain]

O young and noble Cato, are you down?
You're dying now as nobly as Titinius,   10
Worth all the honors due to Cato's son.

[LUCILIUS is captured]

FIRST SOLDIER
Yield, or you die.

LUCILIUS
> To die is why I yield.

> [Gives him money]

There's so much here I know you'll kill me now.
Kill Brutus and be honored by this act.

FIRST SOLDIER
We must not. This prisoner's a noble!   15

SECOND SOLDIER
Make room! Tell Antony, we've taken Brutus.

FIRST SOLDIER
I'll tell him. Look, the general's coming now.

> [Enter MARK ANTONY]

We've captured Brutus, captured him, my lord.

MARK ANTONY
Where is he?

LUCILIUS
Safe, Antony, Brutus is safe enough.   20
I guarantee you that no enemy
Shall ever take alive the noble Brutus.
The gods defend him from so great a shame!
And when you find the man, alive or dead,
You'll find a Brutus true to his own self.   25

MARK ANTONY
This is not Brutus, friend, but I assure you,
A prize no less in worth. Keep this man safe,
Treat him with kindness. I had rather have
Such men as friends than enemies. Go on,
And see if Brutus is alive or dead,   30
And bring back word on how the day turned out.
You'll find me in Octavius' tent.

> [Exit all]

Scene Five. Another Part of the Battlefield

[Enter BRUTUS, DARDANIUS, CLITUS,
STRATO, and VOLUMNIUS]

BRUTUS
Come, poor remaining friends, rest on this rock.

[They rest, with STRATO falling asleep]

CLITUS (a soldier)
Statilius signaled us by torch, my lord,
But hasn't yet come back. He's slain or captured.

BRUTUS
Sit down here, Clitus. "Slay" indeed's the word,
The height of fashion. Now listen to me, Clitus.   5

[BRUTUS whispers to CLITUS]

CLITUS
What, me, my lord? No, not for all the world.

BRUTUS
Silence. No words.

CLITUS
                    I'd rather kill myself.

BRUTUS
Listen, Dardanius.

[BRUTUS whispers to DARDANIUS]

DARDANIUS (a soldier)
                    Would I do such a deed?

CLITUS
O Dardanius!

DARDANIUS
O Clitus!   10

CLITUS
What awful thing did Brutus ask of you?

DARDANIUS
To kill him, Clitus. Look, he's meditating.

CLITUS
This noble vessel's now so full of grief
The overflow runs from his very eyes.

BRUTUS
Come, good Volumnius. I need a word.   15

VOLUMNIUS (a soldier)
My lord, what is it?

BRUTUS
                    Why, this, Volumnius:
The ghost of Caesar has appeared to me
Two separate times at night, at Sardis once,
And just last night here in Philippi's fields.
I know my hour has come.

VOLUMNIUS
                    Not so, my lord.   20

BRUTUS
Yes, I am sure it has, Volumnius.
You see this world, Volumnius, how it's gone.
Our enemies have steered us to the brink.

                [Trumpets sound at a distance]

It's worthier to make the leap ourselves
Than stall until they push us. Good Volumnius,   25
You know that we two went to school together,
So for old friendship's sake, I ask you now,
Hold out my sword, while I run into it.

VOLUMNIUS
That's not a duty for a friend, my lord.

[Louder trumpets sound]

CLITUS
Flee, flee, my lord! There is no staying here.   30

BRUTUS
Farewell to you, and you, and you, Volumnius.
Strato, you have been sleeping all this time.
Farewell to you too, Strato.—Countrymen,
My heart feels joy that all throughout my life
I've found no friend who wasn't true to me.   35
I'll earn much glory from today's defeat,
More than Octavius and Mark Antony
Will gain from conquest so dishonorable.
A final farewell now, for Brutus' tongue
Has almost reached the end of its life story.   40
Night's heavy on my eyes. My bones, which toiled
So long to reach this hour, now wish to rest.

[Trumpets sound. Voices cry, "Flee, flee, flee!"]

CLITUS
Flee, my lord, flee!

BRUTUS
                    Go! I will follow.

[Exit CLITUS, DARDANIUS, and VOLUMNIUS]

Please, Strato, could you stay here with your lord?
You are a fellow who is much esteemed.   45
Your life has shown a hint of honor in it.
Hold out my sword, and turn away your face
While I run into it. Please, do this, Strato.

STRATO (a soldier)
First give me your hand. Fare you well, my lord.

BRUTUS
Farewell, good Strato.

[BRUTUS runs into his sword]

—Caesar, now you sleep,   50
I killed you with a will not half so deep.

[BRUTUS dies]

[Trumpets sound a call to halt. Enter OCTAVIUS,
MARK ANTONY, MESSALA, LUCILIUS, and ARMY]

OCTAVIUS
Whose servant's that?

MESSALA
My master's servant.—Strato, where's your master?

STRATO
Free from the bondage you are in, Messala.
The conquerors can only burn him now,   55
For Brutus overtook himself alone,
And no man else gains honor from his death.

LUCILIUS
That's how he should be found. I thank you, Brutus,
For proving what Lucilius said is true.

OCTAVIUS
All who served Brutus, now are in my service.   60
Fellow, will you spend time in my employ?

STRATO
Yes, if Messala recommends me to you.

OCTAVIUS
Do so, good Messala.

MESSALA
Strato, how did my master die?

STRATO
I held his sword, and he ran into it.   65

MESSALA
Octavius, then he should go with you,
For he's the last of us to serve my master.

MARK ANTONY
This was the noblest Roman of them all.
All the conspirators, except for him,
Were acting out of malice toward great Caesar.   70
He joined them backing honest, selfless goals
And thinking only of the common good.
He led a noble life, his qualities
So balanced even Nature might stand up
And say to all the world, "This was a man!"   75

OCTAVIUS
Let's grant a man of such inherent worth
The honor of a proper burial.
Tonight within my tent his bones shall lie,
A soldier who deserves respect so high.
So, sound the call to cease, and let's make way   80
To share the glories of this happy day.

[Exit]

THE END

Endnotes

Act One
[1] Pompey, Crassus, and Julius Caesar had formed a triumvirate to rule Rome. After Crassus died in 53 BC, Caesar and Pompey began a power struggle and became opponents in a civil war. Caesar defeated Pompey at the battle of Pharsalia in 48 BC and Pompey's sons at the battle of Munda.

[2] The festival, a fertility celebration named for the deity Lupercal, was observed from February 13-15. The festivities included naked men who, carrying a strap made from sacrificed goats, raced around a course lashing as they ran any women who wanted to have their fertility enhanced. Shakespeare, to tighten the action a bit, moves the Lupercalia to March.

[3] In Greek and Roman mythology, Aeneas was a Trojan hero who after the fall of Troy, led a group of survivors to Italy and settled in an area that would become Rome. According to legend, he carried his father Anchises on his back from the burning Troy.

[4] The original line is "Men at some time are masters of their fates." The *Norton Shakespeare* takes at "at some time" to mean "formerly" and changes "are" to "were". Here is a translation if that interpretation is preferred:

Men at one time were masters of their fates.

[5] Marcus Brutus is supposedly descended from Lucius Junius Brutus. According to legend, Brutus drove Tarquinius Superbus, the last of the ancient kings, out of Rome in the sixth century BC.

[6] Marcus Tullius Cicero (106 BC-43 BC) was a philosopher, lawyer, and statesmen. A gifted public speaker and writer, he favored a return to republican government. He had supported Pompey but was careful not to directly oppose Caesar.

[7] The original line is "He should not humor me." Scholars disagree as to whether the "he" refers to Brutus or Caesar.

[8] Around 55 BC, Pompey completed the construction of a large theatre, meeting, and shopping complex. Shakespeare called it Pompey's Porch.

Act Two

[1] Tarquinius Superbus was the last king of Rome. He was overthrown by Lucius Junius Brutus, whom Brutus claims is his ancestor.

[2] Productions have been known to delete lines 175-180 in order to sanitize Brutus' character.

[3] One of several anachronisms in the play.

[4] Marcus Porcius Cato fought with Pompey in the civil war. He committed suicide to avoid capture by Caesar. Brutus comments on Cato's suicide in Act Five.

[5] The original lines read "...and that great men shall press/ For tinctures, stains, relics, and cognizance." Scholars debate the meaning of this odd-looking list. It seems to suggest that nobles will work to stain emblems and tokens of heraldry with a martyr's blood.

Act Three

[1] The First Folio reads "And turn pre-ordinance and first decree/ Into the lane of children." The dispute here concerns the odd use of "lane." Most editors today accept it as a printer's error and substitute "law." And most agree that it refers to the unreliability of children. For *First Folio* aficionados here is a translation that keeps the literal sense of "lane" while implying "narrowness":

> And turn our pre-ordained and settled laws
> Down lanes where children play....

[2] In Latin this means "Even you, Brutus."

[3] Editors have trouble making sense of the original phrase "Our arms in strength of malice," some preferring "unstringed in malice" or even "in strength of amity" or "exempt from malice."

If we imagine a less condensed version of the phrase reading "with the strength our arms can show when they act in malice," Shakespeare is certainly being difficult here, but the line makes some sense. I tried to capture that sense within the constraints imposed by line length and meter.

[4] Shakespeare wants *ambitious* spoken with four-syllables (am-bi-ti-ous) to fill out the meter. I keep it at three syllables but push it a foot further down the line to form a feminine ending (Shakespeare uses this approach later in the scene).

[5] A tribe in the northeastern region of Gaul that Caesar conquered in 57 BC.

Act Four

[1] The original lines read "...I do not doubt/But that my noble master will appear/Such as he is, full of regard and honor." G. L. Kittredge (see the *New Kittredge Shakespeare)* had a different take on it. Here is a translation with his interpretation in mind:

> ....I am sure
> My noble master has behaved in full
> Regard of both your wishes and his honor.

[2] Some scholars feel that Shakespeare intended to delete either the next 16 lines (182-196) or the earlier lines where Brutus discusses Portia's death (146-159). They feel that leaving in both sets of lines requires Brutus to contradict what he told Cassius and pretend that he does not yet know of Portia's death. Brutus' stoic response, however, suggests that he has already given her death some thought and is demonstrating how his stoic philosophy is practiced. Could he be showing off? I'll let the reader decide if one of the sets of lines should go.

Act Five

[1] Epicurus (341 BC – 270 BC), a Greek philosopher, believed that gods did not concern themselves with human affairs and rejected the notion that gods rewarded the good or punished the bad.

Appendix 1: How Iambic Pentameter Works

With the exception of the *Merry Wives of Windsor*, which is 90% prose, Shakespeare's plays employ generous servings of a verse line known as iambic pentameter. Some of his early plays are almost entirely in this form, and all but four plays are at least 50% verse. So it is useful to understand something of iambic pentameter in order to develop an ear for its complex rhythms and to appreciate its dramatic uses.

The term iambic pentameter has three parts which together give a rough description of this verse form. The term *meter* refers to a pattern of rhythm. If you pronounce most two-syllable words in a natural way, you will sense a rhythm, with one syllable receiving more energy than the other. Say the words in (1) and note the different rhythms:

(1)   táble (stressed/unstressed)
       prefér (unstressed/stressed)

An accent mark over a vowel indicates that the syllable containing that vowel is pronounced with more energy than the syllable without the accent mark. We call this increased energy "stress," and an accented syllable is called a stressed syllable. Syllables with less energy are called "unstressed."

Iambic refers to a pattern of meter where an unstressed syllable precedes a stressed syllable. The words in (2) have an iambic rhythm and each forms a metrical unit known as an *iamb*:

(2)   affórd, forbíd, inféct, adópt

Two-word sequences can also have an iambic rhythm.

(3)   a bít, the mán, to gó, is mád, of míne

The term *penta* (five) tells us how many instances of this iambic rhythm make up a line. Each instance is traditionally called a *foot*, so an iambic pentameter line has five iambic feet, or *iambs*. In these ten-syllable lines of five iambs (4), observe how the even-numbered syllables get more stress than the odd numbered syllables.

(4)   Thy gláss/ will shów/ thee hów/ thy béau/ties wéar/
      1   2   3   4   5   6   7 8   9   10
                                              (Sonnet 77, line 1)
      And cáll/ upón/ my sóul/ withín/ the hóuse/
      1   2   3 4   5   6   7 8   9   10
                                          (Twelfth Night, 1.5.251)
      Beshréw/ that héart/ that mákes/ my héart/ to gróan/
      1   2   3   4   5   6   7   8   9 10
                                              (Sonnet 133, line 1)

We sense that the 2nd, 4th, 6th, 8th, and 10th syllables (marked with ´) receive more emphasis than the 1st, 3rd, 5th, 7th, and 9th syllables. In (5), the line has ten syllables, but notice that it is not iambic pentameter. If we use the jargon of verse analysis, we say the line does not *scan*.

(5)   Récog/níze the/ rhýthm's/ nót i/ámbic/
      1 2   3   4   5 6   7 8 9 10

Here the 1st, 3rd, 5th, 7th, and 9th syllables receive the emphasis. If we placed this line after any of the lines in (4), we would not sense a meter developing and would interpret the passage as prose.

(6)   Thy gláss/ will shów/ thee hów/ thy béau/ties wéar/
      Récog/níze the/ rhýthm's/ nót i/ámbic/

One appealing feature of iambic pentameter is that it sounds like verse yet seems natural. The perfectly iambic lines in (7) were randomly selected from different plays. Read them in sequence and notice how they sound rhythmical without seeming "sing-songy" or bouncy.

(7)   Expóse/ thysélf/ to féel/ what wrétch/es féel/
                                          (King Lear, 3.4.39)

In wóm/en's wáx/en héarts/ to sét/ their fórms/
(Twelfth Night, 2.2.30)
To bréathe/ such vóws/ as lóv/ers úse/ to swéar/
(Romeo and Juliet, 2. Prologue. 10)

The three lines, though not sing-songy, do sound rhythmically monotonous. Imagine a play with 2500 such lines pounding away one after the other. The effect would surely be deadening, and dramatists would be severely limited in the kinds of sentences they could write and the vocabulary they could use. So they relax the rules a bit. Most of these deviations fall into two categories: adding extra syllables and altering the iambic meter.

Adding Extra Syllables

There are three common ways to increase the number of syllables beyond ten.

Feminine Endings

If every line had to end with an iamb, many, if not most, two syllable words—*mother, pantry, person, hungry*—could never end a line. So iambic lines allow an extra unstressed eleventh syllable (even a twelfth) at the end of line. This eleventh syllable is called a **feminine ending**, and about 10% of the lines in Shakespeare's early plays and about 30% in his later plays have such endings. The lines from (4) have been modified to show how the feminine ending sounds.

(8) Thy gláss/ will shów/ thee hów/ thy béau/ties wéath**er**/.
    1   2   3   4   5 6   7 8   9   10 Ø
    And cáll upón my sóul withín the pán**try**/
    Beshréw that héart that mákes my héart to súf**fer**/

The words *weather, pantry,* and *suffer* provide the 10th and 11th syllables in these lines, but because the 11th is unstressed, the lines still sound iambic to the trained ear. If feminine endings are allowed, then almost any word can be worked into the end of an iambic pentameter line. In fact, we can easily make the unmetrical line (5) acceptable if we add a syllable at the beginning of the line to push the stressed syllables into the even-numbered positions. Since the 11th syllable is unstressed, it counts as a feminine ending.

(9) *And* réc/ogníze/ the rhýth/m's nót/ iámbic/
    1   2 3 4   5 6   7   8 9 10 Ø

Even without the 11th syllable, adding an extra beat to start the line can restore an iambic rhythm, as *Oh* does here.

(10) Oh, how/ thy worth/ with man/ners may/ I sing/
(Sonnet 39, line 1)

Syllable Deletions
    Lines can also have extra syllables if a syllable can be dropped without the word becoming unintelligible or sounding unnatural. Note how many three-syllable words can become two-syllable words in rapid or slightly slurred speech.

(11)	interest (intrist)	Goneril (gonril)
	monument (mon^yment)	Romeo (romyo)
	traveler (travler)	Juliet (Julyet)
	Viola (vyola)	valiant (valyent)

The trick in "scanning" Shakespeare is to anticipate whether he intends such words to be two or three syllables. My translations of Shakespeare into contemporary English allow such slurring (traditionally called **syncope**). I do, however, avoid slurrings that seem awkward, incomprehensible, or archaic to modern speakers such as *to't* (to it), *e'en* (even), *show'th* (showeth), *upon't* (upon it), and *lov'st* (lovest).

Epic Caesura
    Lines can have an extra unstressed syllable right before a major punctuation break, a variation called **epic caesura** ("says you're a..."). Note in (12) that the second syllable of the word *kingdom* is unstressed and precedes a major punctuation break. This extra eleventh syllable is not added to the syllable count, creating a mid-line feminine ending of sorts.

(12)　　　　　　　Know that we have divided
In three/ our king/**dom**; and 'tis/ our fast/ intent/
1　2　3　4　Ø　5　6　7　8　9 10
(King Lear, 1.1.39-40)

If we allow a feminine ending, slurring, and epic caesura in a single line, we can produce a fairly complex line that stays within the rules of iambic pentameter. How would you scan this thirteen-syllable line (13) from *Twelfth Night*? Is it iambic pentameter?

(13) Even in a minute. So full of shapes is fancy
(Twelfth Night, 1.1.14)

Some scholars question the meter of this line, but here's a try at scanning it. *Even* is slurred to *E'en*. The second, unstressed syllable of *minute* is not counted because it precedes a major punctuation break (epic caesura), and the second, unstressed syllable of *fancy* is a feminine ending.

(14) E'en in/ a min/ute. So full/ of shapes/ is fancy/
　　　 1　2　3　4　Ø　5　6　7　8　9 10 Ø

Shakespeare is pushing the limits here, especially for contemporary speakers who have trouble slurring *even* to *e'en*, but the line technically qualifies as iambic pentameter.

Altering the Meter

Besides an iambic rhythm, a two-syllable foot can have three other rhythms (see the table on page 153). These rhythms can be worked into an iambic pentameter line in various ways.

Spondees

A spondaic foot—one where both syllables are likely to be stressed—can occur anywhere. Spondees work at the beginning of a line as these revisions of the lines from (4) show.

(15) **Bíll's gláss**/ will shów/ thee hów/ thy béau/ties wéar/
Cáll nów/ upón/ my sóul/ withín/ the hóuse/
Cúrse nót/ that héart/ that mákes/ my héart/ to gróan/

Type of Foot	Rhythm	Single Words	Word Sequences
Trochee	stressed/ unstressed	néver, óffer báttle, únder	whát a, wánt to dróp it
Spondee	stressed/ stressed	cúpcáke súitcáse úpkéep	bád lúck tálks bíg
Pyrrhic Foot	unstressed/ unstressed	suit<u>able</u> hap<u>pily</u> list<u>ening</u>	of a, to it, of the

In (16), spondees (in boldface) are worked into the middle and end of lines.

(16) Thy gláss/ will shów/ **Bíll hów**/ thy béau/ties wéar/
Upón/ my sóul/ withín/ the hóuse,/ **cáll nów/**
Beshréw/ that héart/ that mákes/ **Bób's héart**/ to gróan/

Spondees have an interesting effect: they slow down the line. Speakers need time to give stressed syllables extra energy, so lines filled with spondees have a deliberate, pounding rhythm. A line from *King Lear* demonstrates this clearly.

(17) Nó, nó,/ nó, nó!/ Cóme, lét's/ awáy/ to príson/
(King Lear, 5.3.9)

Trochees

If every iambic pentameter line had to begin with an iamb, then most English words could not start a line. Yet a quick look at Shakespeare's sonnets reveals a different reality. We find these poems start with stressed one-syllable words (*look, when, not, but, let, lord, how, why, full, take, sin, thus, love*), and trochaic two-syllable words (*béing, wéary, músic, Cúpid*)—all words or phrases that start off the line with a stressed syllable.

Iambic pentameter solves this problem by allowing a trochaic rhythm to start a line. These modified versions of (4) are all acceptable iambic pentameter lines.

(18) **Mírrors**/ will shów/ thee hów/ thy béau/ties wéar/
    Cálling/ upón/ my sóul/ withín/ the hóuse/
    Cúrsing/ that héart/ that mákes/ my héart/ to gróan/

Trochees can also occur in the middle of a line if they follow a strongly stressed syllable or a major punctuation break. In (19), *haply* has a trochaic rhythm, but it is allowed because it follows a major punctuation break. It also follows the heavily stressed word *all*.

(19) They lóve/ you áll?/ **Háply**/, when I/ shall wéd/
                     (King Lear, 1.1.110)

Phrases that appear to be trochaic are permitted if they fall within a lengthy sequence of one-syllable words. In the 3rd foot of (20), we would normally expect the word *love* to get more emphasis than *which*, yielding the trochaic rhythm *lóve, which*.

(20) A bróth/er's déad/ **lóve, which**/ she would/ kéep frésh/
                    (Twelfth Night, 1.1.30)

This reading sounds like prose. But notice that the word *which* is surrounded by one-syllable words. In this environment, rarely-stressed words such as *the, which, of, is,* and *been* can be stressed to preserve an iambic rhythm without sounding unnatural, as in (21).

(21) A bróth/er's déad/ love, whích/ she wóuld/ keep frésh/

Actors may choose not to give the line an iambic rhythm, but the fact that they can qualifies the line as iambic pentameter.

Pyrrhic Feet

Normally, pyrrhic feet do not cause a problem. A foot with two unstressed syllables glides right by without upsetting the meter. The lines in (22) show typical uses of pyrrhic feet (in bold italics).

(22) For she/ did speak/ in starts/ distract/**edly**/
    She loves/ me sure./ The cun/**ning of**/ her passion/
    Invites/ in me/ this chur/lish mes/**senger**. /
                 (Twelfth Night, 2.2.20-22)

Unmetrical Lines

If trochaic, spondaic, and pyrrhic feet can come anywhere in a line, then wouldn't just about any ten-syllable line be iambic pentameter? Actually, the meter is more restricted than it appears because of one rule: a word with a trochaic rhythm cannot fill the 2nd, 3rd, 4th, or 5th foot unless a stressed syllable or a major punctuation break precedes that foot. Sounds complicated, but that is the rule violated by the italicized sequence in (23).

(23) Áfter/ *dínner/* he wálked/ acróss/ the stréet/
         1   2   3   4   5   6   7 8   9   10

The *-ter* of *after* and the first syllable of the trochaic word *dínner* cannot be in two separate feet because that leaves the stressed syllable of *dinner* in an odd-numbered position surrounded by two unstressed syllables. Forcing the two-syllable word *dinner* into an iambic rhythm is too unnatural, something on the order of *d'nér*. To fix this line, we need to force the first syllable of *dinner* into an even-numbered position. Here are several possibilities.

(24) He áft/er dín/ner wálked/ acróss/ the róad/
      He wálked/ 'cross th' róad/ right áf/ter dín/ner, sír/

The second line requires two elisions—*'cross* and *th' road.* My translations avoid odd-looking elisions like *th' road,* but be ready for them if you delve into the original. Can you figure out these? *Woo't, 'a, s', to't, tak'n, sev'n, within's.* (Answers: *wouldst thou, he, his, to it, taken, seven, within this*).

Regardless of what precedes it, we rarely find a word with a trochaic rhythm filling the last foot. Line (25), like (23), is unmetrical and interpreted as prose, not verse.

(25) He wálked/ acróss/ the róad/ to éat /*dínner/*

Line (25) can be corrected if we force a feminine ending by adding an extra syllable, in this case the word *his.*

(26) He wálked/ acróss/ the róad/to éat/his dínner/
        1   2   3   4   5 6   7 8   9   10   Ø

To highlight the difference between verse and prose, let's mechanically divide a prose passage from *King Lear* into ten-syllable lines. Even with slurring and long lines, only the lines in **bold italics** seem acceptable iambic pentameter, and some of these require uncharacteristic and rather clumsy breaks in the syntax at the end of lines. The other lines all deviate from Shakespeare's usual verse.

(27) **EDMUND**
This is the exc'llent fopp'ry of the world
That, when we are sick in fortune—often
The surfeit of our own behaviour—we
Make guilty of our disasters the sun,
The moon, and the stars; as if we were villains
On necessity; fools by heavenly
Compulsion; knaves, thieves, and treachers by spherical
Pre-dominance; drunkards, liars, and adulterers
By an enforcéd obedience of
Planetary influence; and all that
We are evil in, by a divine thrusting
On: an admirable evasion of whoremaster
Man, to lay his goatish disposition
To the charge of a star! My father compounded
With my mother under the dragon's tail
And my nativity was under Ursa
Major; so that it follows I am rough
***And lecherous.—Tut!** I should have been that*
I am, had the maidenliest star in
The firmament twinkled on my bastardizing.
                              (King Lear, 1.2.125-140)

All told, only five out of twenty lines can be read as verse, and that is why Edmund's speech is always formatted as prose.

Let's compare Edmund's prose soliloquy to a passage that certainly complicates the iambic pattern yet is always formatted as verse. I have highlighted with **bold italics** some of the more difficult lines to scan.

(27) **LEAR**
Peace, Kent!
Come not between the dragon and his wrath.

I lov'd her most, and thought to set my rest
On her kind nursery—Hence, and avoid my sight!
So be my grave my peace, as here I give
Her father's heart from her!   Call France—who stirs?
Call Burgundy!—Cornwall and Albany,
With my two daughters' dowers digest this third:
               [*dowers* is slurred to one-syllable]
Let pride, which she calls plainness, marry her.
I do invest you jointly in my power,
Pre-eminence, and all the large effects
That troop with majesty.—Ourself, by monthly course,
               [long line]
With reservation of an hundred knights,
By you to be sustain'd, shall our abode
Make with you by due turns. Only we still retain
[long]
The name, and all th' additions to a king;
The sway, revénue, execution of the rest,   [long]
Belovèd sons, be yours; which to confirm,
This coronet part betwixt you....[*coronet* slurred]

KENT
                              Royal Lear,
                              (King Lear, 1.1.135-155)

   This passage is about as wild as Shakespeare's iambic
pentameter gets, yet only five of the eighteen lines are difficult
to scan. Three are long lines (hexameters), more frequent in
Shakespeare's later plays, and the other two deviant lines have
rather complicated rhythms, perhaps to signal that Lear is
yelling and losing his temper. The last line is an example of a
shared line where one speaker finishes the line by responding
to or overlapping the previous speaker.
   This comparison shows that iambic pentameter is not
prose and that verse dramatists are quite aware when they are
shifting between verse and prose (even if many modern actors
obscure the difference). It also shows that iambic pentameter,
while it allows for deviation in line length and rhythm, imposes
constraints on a line. My translations honor these constraints

and aim to preserve in contemporary English the rhythm of Shakespeare's verse.

Scanning Exercise

Here is the untranslated version of Duke Orsino's famous opening speech in *Twelfth Night*. Scholars have argued that the meter is as fickle and impulsive as the Duke himself, with smooth, flowing phrases interrupted by spondaic rhythms. Try scanning it. You should find at least one example of all the metrical variations described above. I have added several stress marks to show how Shakespeare most likely pronounced the words.

DUKE ORSINO

If music be the food of love, play on.
Give me excéss of it, that, súrfeiting,
The appetite may sicken and so die.
That strain again! It had a dying fall.
O, it came o'er my ear like the sweet sound
That breathes upon a bank of violets,
Stealing and giving odour. Enough; no more.
'Tis not so sweet now as it was before.
O spirit of love, how quick and fresh art thou!
That, notwithstanding thy capacity
Receiveth as the sea, nought enters there,
Of what validity and pitch soé'er,
But falls into abatement and low price,
Even in a minute. So full of shapes is fancy
That it alone is high fantastical.

Appendix 2: The Globe and the Case for Translation

Follow him, friends. We'll hear a play tomorrow.
(Hamlet, Act 2, Scene 2)

You complain about the difficulty of Shakespeare's plays and some knowing type says, "You can't appreciate Shakespeare's work by reading it on the page. Shakespeare wrote for the stage, and you must see his works performed to appreciate them fully. The actors, through their facial expressions, costuming, and gestures, will provide the necessary context to make the plays meaningful."

Armed with such reassurance and confident that the actors at your local Shakespeare company will give you all the help you need, you head off to a production of *Henry V*. After a prologue in which a charming fellow tells you "Gently to hear, kindly to judge, our play," two men enter to catch us up on what's troubling King Henry's realm.

Man Dressed Like a Monk
My lord, I'll tell you, that self bill is urged
Which in th' eleventh year of the last king's reign
Was like, and had indeed against us passed,
But that the scambling and unquiet time
Did push it out of farther question.

Another Man Dressed Like a Monk
But how, my lord, shall we resist it now?

Fifteen seconds into the play, panic sets in. But you remember some more advice. "It's not important that you understand every word. Relax and just try to catch the gist." All right, let's try that. But first you desperately scan the program to find out who these two characters are. They called each other "my lord," but they are dressed like monks. Ah, they are bishops.

158

Now you can relax a little. But while doing this research, the bishops have pushed ahead. You pick up this bit of exposition from one of the bishops:

> ...And the mute wonder lurketh in men's ears
> To steal his sweet and honeyed sentences;
> So that the art and practic part of life
> Must be the mistress to this theoric
> Which is a wonder how his Grace should glean it,
> Since his addiction was to courses vain....

Now even the gist is slipping away. And the actor, though he seems quite concerned about something, is not particularly expressive and does not gesture much, perhaps because his costume is so baggy. Wait, just relax.

> ...Upon our spiritual convocation
> And in regard of causes now in hand
> Which I have opened to his Grace at large
> As touching France, to give a greater sum
> Than ever at one time the clergy yet
> Did to his predecessors part withal.

Check your watch. If they keep talking this fast, the play can't last more than three hours.

The problem is you are armed with wishful thinking, not helpful advice. No amount of expressive acting on the actors' part or relaxation on your part can substitute for actually understanding what the characters say. Try this test. Watch a TV sitcom with the sound turned down. Choose a sitcom because, like Shakespeare, sitcoms use dialog, rather than physical action, to carry the story along. With the sound down, you probably know who is happy, sad, angry, and so forth, but you won't get any of the jokes or learn much about the characters' thinking or motives. Then turn up the sound and listen to the show from another room. Of course, you'll miss out on the funny faces they make and any slapstick, but you will understand the basic plot and conflicts and catch many of the jokes.

Is attending a Shakespeare play too much like watching

a sitcom with the sound turned down? If so, then we English speakers cannot appreciate what drove people to the theatre in Shakespeare's day and why people around the world who speak little or no English continue to marvel at his accomplishments. Shakespeare is not world famous because his plays were written in 400-year-old English. He is famous because his plays work brilliantly on the stage and are packed full of a rich variety of characters who say interesting things in vivid, metrically interesting language. And that language has been magnificently recreated in comprehensible translations in many of the world's languages. Certainly contemporary English can join the list of languages where Shakespeare is fully understood by the casual reader or theatre patron.

Enter the Globe

The design of outdoor theatres in Shakespeare's day argues for comprehensible texts. The most famous of these theatres, the Globe, was the primary venue for Shakespeare's plays from its opening in 1599 until it burned down in 1613. All told, Shakespeare wrote fifteen plays for that stage, with revivals of at least six earlier plays. Other venues staged his plays as well, including courts and indoor theatres. But the Globe and similar theatres—the Swan, the Rose, and the Fortune—were home to many great successes of the Elizabethan stage.

Since no theatres from Shakespeare's time have survived, our knowledge of the Globe is limited to archaeological evidence, sketches, and eyewitness descriptions. By using this evidence along with imaginative back-engineering, architects, scholars, and theatre experts have rebuilt the Globe Theatre in London along the south bank of the Thames River not far from the site of the original Globe. This theatre, a long-time dream of actor/director Sam Wanamaker (1919-1993) and architect Theo Crosby (1925-1994), officially opened in 1997 and is a working theatre offering live productions and guided tours.

The structure of this close facsimile of the Globe sheds new light on how Shakespeare's plays must have played to the audience. The Globe is a nearly round building with three tiers of seating in the shape of a round horseshoe (see Figure 1). The ends of the horseshoe connect to a three-story building called

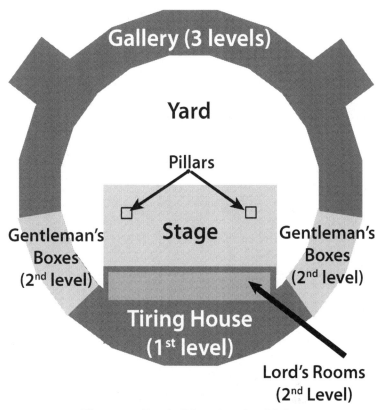

Figure 1; Basic Plan for the Globe

the Tiring House (from "attire"), which includes the backstage area and the dressing rooms.

The stage is large, about 1100 square feet, and is almost twice as wide as it is deep. The backdrop for the stage is the Tiring House itself (see Figure 2). The bottom story has three doors, the middle one curtained, allowing entrance to the stage from the backstage area. The second story is a balcony where actors or musicians can perform. It also has space for seating. Above this second level, a roof extends over the stage supported by two pillars that are about halfway across the stage in front of the side doors. Called the "heavens," this roof is painted with the sun, the moon, and stars. Above the stage roof toward the back is an A-frame structure that resembles a small house. This structure can be used to produce sound effects such as thunder, trumpet blasts, and cannon fire. The stage floor has trapdoors used for special effects.

The main seating area is typical of Elizabethan outdoor theatres and is based on the Roman amphitheatre with its stacked galleries. The three galleries, one directly on top of the other, stretch uniformly around the horseshoe with seating for about 900 people on benches. Every 12 feet or so, an 8-10 inch support post blocks the view of the seats behind it. A thatched roof protects the galleries, but the area between the galleries and the stage is open to the air. The open area in the roof provides the only source of light.

With the galleries forming a fairly large circle and the stage elevated 5 feet, there is an open area around the stage with room for hundreds of people to stand without blocking the view of those seated in the lower gallery. In Shakespeare's day, this

Figure 2: Basic Layout of the Globe Stage

standing-room-only crowd—the "groundlings"—could attend the play for the price of a penny.

The pillars on the stage supporting the "heavens" are both a resource and a problem. They can serve as props, standing in for a forest or a hiding place, but they also block the view of part of the stage from all seating and standing locations. And because the Tiring House juts out into the arena, some seats offer a view of as little as 25% of the stage. In other words, no seat in the Globe offers a complete view of the stage, and many offer a highly restricted view.

The first assumption may be that the designers of the globe

This 19th century engraving imagines the 1613 Globe as a six-sided building taller than it is wide. The rebuilt Globe has 20 sides and a diameter that is double its highest point.

were incompetent until we see what happens when a play is performed. The Globe is not designed for watching a play up close. The stage itself is too large for that. It is designed for listening to a play, and performances today reveal that voices on that stage carry well. It turns out that the Elizabethan theatre designers must have thought a lot about acoustics and incorporated that knowledge into their designs. It is notable that while no seat is particularly close to the stage, the farthest seat is no more than 65 feet or so from the center of the stage, well within easy shouting distance. Shakespeare's own words remind us that plays were to be heard. The Prologue of *Romeo and Juliet* promises the playgoer that

> ...if you with patient ears attend,
> What here shall miss, our toil shall strive to mend.

Scholars disagree as to what the actors are promising—whether to fix the dialog in future performances or to fill in with strong performances what the words don't capture—but the lines clearly encourage close listening. We already saw that the prologue to *Henry V* humbly requests the audience to "hear" the play.

This is not to say that there was nothing to see, for everything about the Globe suggests color, extravaganza, epic, and shared audience experience. The actors wore elaborate costumes, and the theatre was decorated with brightly colored, even tacky, carvings and trim. The stage was big enough to stage sword fights and dances. And as with arena seating today, the customers, sitting in what Shakespeare called "this wooden O," were very aware of the other members of the audience, whose faces and attire were in plain view and part of the spectacle. No doubt those seated in the Lords' rooms and Gentleman's boxes, located behind the stage, were more interested in being seen than seeing.

This is also not to say that Elizabethan audiences were perfectly attentive. In fact, the natural restlessness of the audience may account for why Shakespeare's language is so lexically rich and so rhythmically and syntactically intoxicating. The sound of the language itself commands our attention. Plus the theatre's layout may help enforce silence since those prone to talking and

The rebuilt Globe forms a circle with a diameter of about 99 feet. It has two stairwells on the outside to reach the upper galleries. The walls are made of plaster and oak. The roof is thatched.

heckling can see disapproving faces. Bored spectators can keep entertained by studying the crowd.

The Globe's design allows for the visual but ultimately argues against the notion that "seeing" a play is what Shakespeare is all about. Elizabethan drama had little scenery and limited props with no formal announcement of scene locations. Understanding Shakespeare did not require a perfect view of the stage or close-ups of actors' faces. It required listening for hints in the dialog that suggest setting and identify characters. It required actors with loud, clear voices and a quiet theatre. Today, even with a quiet house and highly trained, full-throated actors, attentive listening is not enough. Nuanced understanding is a struggle not because the actors speak too fast or because English teachers are not doing their job but because the archaic language has too many unfamiliar elements.

Let's go back to *Henry V.* The longwinded Archbishop of Canterbury, now deep into a 63-line discourse, says,

...So that, as clear as is the summer's sun...

Somebody two rows away laughs. The Archbishop continues,

> ...King Pepin's title and Hugh Capet's claim,
> King Lewis his satisfaction, all appear
> To hold in right and title of the female;
> So do the kings of France unto this day,
> Howbeit, they would hold up this Salique Law
> To bar your Highness claiming from the female,
> And rather choose to hide them in the net
> Than amply to imbar their crooked titles
> Usurped from you and your progenitors.

Did he say Sally Claw? Your mind has wandered, but you still have hopes of grabbing some of the gist. It seems some French kings helped a female who goes by the name of Sally Claw to usurp King Henry's title. Well, you're wrong. Sally hasn't usurped anything. In fact, there is no Sally. The true usurper here—O you with patient ears—is time and language change. Those two have usurped our title to full comprehension of Shakespeare's words and turned enjoyment into frustration. Careful translation can return this title to the rightful owners—those who speak the English we use today.

from *Julius Caesar*, Act Five

Sources

Editions of the Play

The Annotated Shakespeare. 2006. Burton Raffel, ed. New Haven and London: Yale University Press.

The Arden Shakespeare. 1998. David Daniell, ed. London: Thomson Learning.

The New Kittredge Shakespeare. 2008. George L. Kittredge and Sarah Hatchuel, eds. Newburyport, MA: Focus Publishing.

The New Cambridge Shakespeare. 1988, 2003. Marvin Spevack. Cambridge: Cambridge University Press.

The Folger Shakespeare Library. 1992. Barbara A. Mowat and Paul Werstine, eds. New York: Washington Square Press.

The Norton Shakespeare: Based on the Oxford Edition, 2nd Edition. 2008, 1997. S. Greenblatt, W. Cohen, J. E. Howard, and K. E. Maus, eds. New York and London: W.W. Norton & Co.

Oxford School Shakespeare. 1979, 2001. Roma Gill, ed. Oxford: Oxford University Press.

The Oxford Shakespeare. 1984. Arthur Humphreys, ed. Oxford: Oxford University Press.

The RSC Shakespeare. 2007. Jonathan Bate and Eric Rasmussen, eds. New York: The Modern Library.

The Riverside Shakespeare. 1997. Boston and New York: Houghton Mifflin Company.

Signet Classics. 1963, 1986. William and Barbara Rosen, ed. New York: New American Library.

Other Sources

Abbott, E. A. *A Shakespearian Grammar*. 2003. Mineola, New York: Dover Publications, Inc.

Crystal, David and Ben Crystal. *Shakespeare's Words: A Glossary and Language Companion*. 2002. London: Penguin Books.

Compact Edition of the Oxford English Dictionary. 1971. Oxford University Press.

Onions, C.T. *A Shakespeare Glossary*. 1986. Revised and enlarged by Robert D. Eagleson.

Schmidt, Alexander. 1971. *Shakespeare Lexicon and Quotation Dictionary, Volumes 1 and 2*. New York: Dover Publications.

Facts About Julius Caesar

Shakespeare's 20th play (or so)

First performed in 1599

About 5% prose, with 2,149 blank verse lines, 35 epic caesurae, 108 short lines, and 21 long lines (according to *Shakespeare's Metrical Art* by George T. Wright).

No songs though Brutus requests music in Act Four.

The *Internet Movie Database* lists 21 filmed versions where Shakespeare gets writing credit, including 5 films from the silent era. A big budget version in 1953, directed by Joseph Mankiewicz, featured Marlon Brando as Mark Antony, with James Mason, John Gielgud, and Deborah Kerr. Charlton Heston played Mark Antony on film twice, in 1950 and 1970.

52 characters with lines. Just 2 female parts.

Story Credit
The primary source was Thomas North's translation of *Plutarch's Lives of the Most Noble Grecians and Romans* (1579). Plutarch wrote these biographies in the late 1st century.

Continuity problems?
In Act Four, Brutus is informed of the death of Portia twice. Some feel one of the announcements needs to be cut.

Anachronisms
The characters refer to time kept by mechanical clocks, which were invented much later.
The clothing seems to be Elizabethan dress rather than Roman attire, including "sweaty nightcaps."
Brutus is reading a modern book in Act Four. The original play describes "a leaf turned down."
(This translation obscures the clothing and book anachronisms somewhat.)

Made in the USA
Lexington, KY
05 September 2015